More Praise for *Full Steam Ahead!*

"Inspiring a shared vision is *the* signature leadership competency. It's also the most difficult practice to learn and apply. In this wonderful gem of a book, Ken Blanchard and Jesse Stoner show you how to find a meaningful purpose, picture a compelling future, and clarify your values. This engaging story is full of practical advice that you'll be able to apply immediately. It's essential reading for any leader who needs to answer the question, 'Where are we going?' Come to think of it, that would be all of us!"

—**Jim Kouzes, coauthor of the bestselling *The Leadership Challenge* and *The Truth About Leadership* and Dean's Executive Professor of Leadership, Leavey School of Business.**

"So many of the lessons I share with my teams revolve around attaining goals by having a clear vision of where we are headed as a group and also individually. *Full Steam Ahead!* emphasizes the ways in which those visions can not only help you reach greatness but also maintain it for you and your team. In the past I've shared this book with friends and coaching peers alike and continue to do so in order to share the wisdom and effective guidance that Ken and Jesse provide on each and every page."

—**John Calipari, Head Coach, University of Kentucky Men's Basketball, two-time Naismith Men's College Coach of the Year, and author of the national bestseller *Bounce Back***

"I LUV this heartwarming lesson from Blanchard and Stoner and urge anyone who wants to develop a clear vision to study the messages clearly and articulately delivered on each page of *Full Steam Ahead!*"

—**Colleen Barrett, President Emeritus, Southwest Airlines Company, and coauthor of *Lead with LUV***

"In order to do your personal best, you must have a vision. To me a clear vision answers the question, 'What mountain do we want to climb?' *Full Steam Ahead!* is a wonderful guidebook that will not only help you find your mountain but give you all the road maps and tools you'll need to make it to the top. Highly recommended!"

—**Garry Ridge, CEO, WD-40 Company, and coauthor of *Helping People Win at Work***

"A clear vision gives an organization heart. Without it, work will have no meaning. *Full Steam Ahead!* is a must-read."
—**James H. Amos, Jr., Chairman Emeritus, Mail Boxes Etc.**

"Before beginning any kind of planning, everyone on the team should read this book. It will ensure you're headed in the right direction. *Full Steam Ahead!* should be required reading."
—**Barbara Bennett, former Executive Vice President, The Stanley Works**

"Leadership is about going somewhere. Without a clear vision your leadership doesn't matter. *Full Steam Ahead!* will help your leadership efforts get started in the right direction."
—**James E. Despain, former Vice President, Caterpillar, and coauthor of *And Dignity for All***

"Great things come from a powerful vision—fortunes are made, diseases get cured, and democracies are born. Blanchard and Stoner teach readers not only how to develop a potent vision in *Full Steam Ahead!* but also how to bring it alive in the hearts and minds of the people who will make it happen."
—**Robert W. Jacobs, author of *Real Time Strategic Change***

"Blanchard and Stoner demonstrate how clear vision helps you focus on the results you desire. Time is a precious commodity. *Full Steam Ahead!* shows you how to get the most out of your efforts."
—**Loyal Nordstrom, President, Honolulu Holdings, Inc.**

Full Steam Ahead!

FULL STEAM AHEAD!

SECOND EDITION

Unleash the Power of Vision in Your Work and Your Life

Ken Blanchard
Jesse Lyn Stoner

BK

Berrett–Koehler Publishers, Inc.
San Francisco
a BK Business book

Berrett-Koehler Publishers, Inc.
235 Montgomery, Suite 650
San Francisco, CA 94104-2916
Tel: (415) 288-0260   Fax: (415) 362-2512   www.bkconnection.com

Ordering Information

Quantity sales. Special discounts are available on quantity purchases by corporations, associations, and others. For details, contact the "Special Sales Department" at the Berrett-Koehler address above.

Individual sales. Berrett-Koehler publications are available through most bookstores. They can also be ordered directly from Berrett-Koehler: Tel: (800) 929-2929; Fax: (802) 864-7626; www.bkconnection.com

Orders for college textbook/course adoption use. Please contact Berrett-Koehler: Tel: (800) 929-2929; Fax: (802) 864-7626.

Orders by U.S. trade bookstores and wholesalers. Please contact Ingram Publisher Services, Tel: (800) 509-4887; Fax: (800) 838-1149; E-mail: customer.service@ingram publisherservices.com; or visit www.ingrampublisherservices.com/Ordering for details about electronic ordering.

Berrett-Koehler and the BK logo are registered trademarks of Berrett-Koehler Publishers, Inc.

Printed in the United States of America

Berrett-Koehler books are printed on long-lasting acid-free paper. When it is available, we choose paper that has been manufactured by environmentally responsible processes. These may include using trees grown in sustainable forests, incorporating recycled paper, minimizing chlorine in bleaching, or recycling the energy produced at the paper mill.

Production management: Michael Bass Associates

Cover design: Richard Adelson

Library of Congress Cataloging-in-Publication Data
Blanchard, Kenneth H.
    Full steam ahead! : unleash the power of vision in your work and in your life / Ken Blanchard and Jesse Lyn Stoner.
        p. cm.
    ISBN 978-1-60509-875-3
    1. Goal (Psychology) 2. Leadership. 3. Strategic planning 4. Mission statements. 5. Organizational effectiveness. I. Stoner, Jesse, 1949– II. Title.
    BF505.G6B536 2011
    650.1—dc21

                                                              2010053669
                                                              CIP

Second Edition
15   14   13   12   11   10   9   8   7   6   5   4   3   2   1

To my children Michael and Noah,
who have added a richness I never could have
imagined to my own personal vision.

—JESSE LYN STONER

To Scott and Debbie
and the wonderful grandchildren they've given us:
Alec, Kyle, Kurtis, Atticus, and Hannah.
They help me move full steam ahead!

—KEN BLANCHARD

Contents

Foreword

I'm not going to lie to you. Many sophisticated readers will be tempted to dismiss this wonderful little book. To them, the lessons will seem simple, even obvious, and the storylike manner in which it is told might come across as homey.

But as they keep reading, something will hit them. "You know, this stuff makes all the sense in the world." And not long after that, something else will hit them. "Hey, I'm not doing half of this stuff that makes all the sense in the world!" If they have enough humility and genuine desire to make their lives better, they'll start taking Ken Blanchard and Jesse Stoner's advice and watch their organizations and families be transformed.

Once again, though, I'm going to be honest. I think the reason some people might be reluctant to implement these ideas is fear. Maybe they don't see themselves as capable of acting like Jim or Ellie—the main characters in the story—people who are passionate, emotional, even vulnerable. Maybe they had a vision in the past that failed to materialize, and now they're afraid that creating an emotionally and intellectually compelling vision will be met with skepticism or, worse, cynicism.

And I don't blame people for having those fears, because they're reasonable ones. Anyone who wants to create a transformation—in either one's personal or professional life—will have to face the distinct possibility of rejection. But for those who do face and overcome that fear, who extract the lessons from this wonderfully powerful and simple book and put them into practice, the rewards will be extraordinary.

So I guess the only question that remains for those who are holding this book in their hands right now is "Which type of person are you?" I hope you'll have the courage, humility, and wisdom to read on and become the visionary leader that our world so desperately needs.

PATRICK LENCIONI
President of The Table Group and
author of *The Five Dysfunctions of a Team*

Preface

We are thrilled that our publisher, Berrett-Koehler, has asked us to write a second edition of *Full Steam Ahead!* It is one of the most important books we have been involved with over the years. The first edition was an international best seller, translated into twenty-two foreign languages. We're delighted that the book has touched so many people.

In our work with organizations worldwide, we have observed that the biggest impediment to managers becoming great leaders is the lack of a clear vision—knowing who you are (your purpose), where you're going (your picture of the future), and what will guide your journey (your values). Yet less than 10 percent of the organizations we have visited are led by managers who have a clear sense of where they are trying to lead people.

Lack of a clear vision is a problem because vision is the starting point of all leadership. After all, leadership is about going somewhere. If leaders are not working toward a shared vision, their leadership can become self-serving and, ultimately, fail.

Most of the people we talk with agree that vision is important. They know that without a clear vision, they are inundated with demands for their time that can pull them off focus and waste a lot of energy. They recognize the negative effect of lack of a vision, but they are unsure of how to create one. Yet in many organizations where a vision statement does exist, it turns people off. The statement may be found framed on walls, but it provides no guidance or, worse, has nothing to do with the reality of how things actually are.

If you have never had a vision—or if you have made a failed attempt to create one—this updated edition of *Full Steam Ahead!* can help you succeed. We have brought this seemingly complex subject down to earth, making it simple to understand and easy to apply.

In this expanded edition, we have added a chapter on sustainability, provided more detail on how to implement a vision, included more information on creating a team vision, and provided a new resource section at the end of the book that includes an assessment and game plan for creating a shared vision.

Whether you're an individual seeking to live a meaningful life, a member or leader of a team, or the head of a multinational corporation wanting to guide your organization, understanding the key elements of a vision will help you manifest your dreams.

Yet this book is about more than merely creating a compelling vision. It's also about making sure that your vision is shared, that it comes alive and continues to guide you on a day-by-day basis. Creating a vision statement is not just a one-time activity. As this book shows, visioning is a lifelong journey.

Whether it's for you personally—or for your family, project, team, department, organization, or community, we hope you will apply these ideas right away, so that you can move full steam ahead!

KEN BLANCHARD
JESSE LYN STONER

A Proper Ending

I stood in disbelief as a cold wind lashed across my face. *I can't believe he's gone*, I thought. I couldn't imagine a world without Jim in it. Yet, here I stood at an open grave on this gloomy winter day. I looked around at those gathered with me. They appeared to be as shocked as I felt. Jim had meant so much to all of us.

As Jim's daughter Kristen read the eulogy, the familiar words comforted me, and I could almost sense his presence.

"Jim Carpenter was a loving teacher and example of simple truths, whose leadership helped him and others awaken to the presence of God in their lives. He was a caring child of God, a son, brother, spouse, father, grandfather, father-in-law, brother-in-law, godfather, uncle, cousin, friend, and business colleague, who strove to find a balance between success and significance. He was able to say no in a loving manner to people and projects that got him off purpose. He was a person of high energy who was able to see the positive in any event or situation. No matter what happened, he could find a 'learning' or a message in it. Jim valued integrity; his actions were consistent with his words; and he was a mean, lean, 185-pound, flexible golfing machine. He will be missed because wherever he went, he made the world a better place by his having been there."

A loving teacher and example of simple truths. I reflected how eloquently those words described the way Jim had lived his life. This was the essence of who he was. I smiled to myself as I thought about how the words even captured Jim's humor. He certainly loved golf, even though he had never become a "mean, lean golfing machine."

As we walked away from the cemetery, I caught up with Kristen.

"That was a lovely eulogy," I told her as I put my arm around her.

Kristen sighed and said, "Thanks, Ellie. But I didn't write it. I think Dad did. I was sitting at his desk in his study, trying to compose a eulogy, when I found this one lying in the top drawer. I thought it described him better than anything I could have written."

She paused a moment and continued, "But I don't know *why* he would have written it."

"I know why," I replied softly. "I was with him when he wrote it. He didn't write it for his funeral. It was his vision for his life. It guided him."

Continuing on my own as I headed toward my car, I reflected on Jim's vision. I considered how he had used the power of vision to transform the small insurance agency his father had started into a thriving, nationally recognized company. I chuckled to myself as I remembered how he had struggled at first, knowing he needed a vision but unsure how to create one. He wasn't one of the lucky people who woke up one morning with a clear vision. Yet by understanding the key elements of a vision and what was important about the process of creating, communicating, and living it, he'd been able to create a shared vision that unified and mobilized the people in his agency. Equally important, he had created a vision for his life. And I thought about how I had used those same lessons to create a vision for my life.

Then my thoughts raced back to the beginning of the journey—a journey that had transformed not only the agency but also both of us, so many years ago. It had been a different time, a different life, a different me—yet it felt as though it were only yesterday.

A Real Beginning

I stood before the doors of Carpenter Insurance Agency, at the threshold of a new world. At thirty-eight years old, I had never worked a day outside the house. I had been a top student in college, heading toward a rewarding career. During a summer internship at an accounting firm, I'd met Doug, a handsome, up-and-coming CPA. Our plan was to marry as soon as I graduated. Then I'd go to graduate school, earn an MBA, and get a great job. We'd have a couple of children, and with our two incomes we'd have a large house, a nanny, fun vacations, and a great life.

We did marry and I did begin an MBA program at a prestigious school. But two things happened that weren't in the plan: we got pregnant unexpectedly—twins, no less!—and Doug got sick. Shortly before the twins were born, Doug started coming home from work exhausted. At first we thought he was experiencing "sympathy pregnancy" symptoms. But when muscle weakness and cramps started interfering with his tennis game, he decided to see a doctor. After months of tests, specialists, and anxiety, Doug was diagnosed with ALS (Lou Gehrig's Disease). By the time the twins were eighteen months old, I was a widow.

Snap your fingers and that's how fast fifteen years went by. Fortunately, Doug had a good life insurance policy and his parents helped out, so by living frugally, I was able to stay home with my children full-time. Maybe I felt like I needed to make up for their not having a father, but my children became the center of my life. I dated a bit, but whenever things started getting serious, I'd start feeling disloyal to Doug's memory and to his parents who were helping us out so much.

Now I was at a new point in my life. My children had started high school and didn't seem to need me the way they once had. The years had eased the pain of losing Doug, and the life insurance money was running out. It was time to get a job. And I was ready to start a new life. I had spent the last fifteen years taking care of everyone else. Now it was time to take care of me.

I perused ads for a business or financial position, since that had been my college major. Eventually, I found my first job in the accounting department for this good-sized insurance agency. With a bit of trepidation and a lot of excitement, I went shopping for business clothes and prepared to enter this strange new world.

• • •

As I entered the doors of Carpenter Insurance, I was greeted by Marsha, head of accounting, who had interviewed me for the position. She gave me a tour of the building, outlined my responsibilities, introduced me to my coworkers, handed me some employment paperwork to complete, and showed me my cubicle. A computer had already been set up for me as well as voice mail. There was even a message waiting for me on voice mail:

Good morning, everyone. This is Jim. It's said that Abraham Lincoln often slipped out of the White House on Wednesday evenings to listen to the sermons of Dr. Finnes Gurley at New York Avenue Presbyterian Church. He generally preferred to come and go unnoticed. So when Dr. Gurley knew the president was coming, he left his study door open.

On one of those occasions, the president slipped through a side door in the church and took a seat in the minister's study, located just to the side of the sanctuary. There he propped the door open, just wide enough to hear Dr. Gurley.

During the walk home, an aide asked Mr. Lincoln his appraisal of the sermon. The president thoughtfully replied, "The content was excellent; he delivered with elegance; he obviously put work into the message."

"Then you thought it was an excellent sermon?" questioned the aide.

"No," Lincoln answered.

"But you said that the content was excellent. It was delivered with eloquence, and it showed how hard he worked," the aide pressed.

"That's true," Lincoln said, "But Dr. Gurley forgot the most important ingredient. He forgot to ask us to do something great."

I believe there is nothing wrong with average lives and average accomplishments; most of the good of the world builds on the accumulated efforts of everyday people. But a life should strive for greatness, as Lincoln seemed to know.

Who was Jim, and why was his message in my voice mailbox? This was something I hadn't expected in the business world.

Later in the morning, Marsha explained that I would spend the day shadowing my new coworker, Darryl, who would help me learn the ropes.

I joined Darryl and a few others from the department for lunch. Darryl was quiet, but the rest of us chatted about an upcoming big project, the weather, and our families. I didn't ask about the voice mail message—partly because it slipped my mind but mostly because I didn't want to sound as though I didn't know about the business world.

Although not very social, Darryl was a good person to explain how things worked because he was so totally task focused. The day flew by and I hardly had time to organize my desk.

• • •

Over the next few days, I dug right in. I was eager to learn everything as quickly as possible. One of Darryl's responsibilities was to collect and organize receipts from the agents for their reimbursable expenses such as travel. He wanted me to take over this responsibility and some others as soon as possible and kept me quite busy. By Friday, I still hadn't asked anyone about the voice mail messages. But each morning, I was intrigued by the brief message that began with the words "Good morning, everyone. This is Jim."

The messages were quite unusual. They seemed to be a mix of stories, personal philosophy, and information about things that were happening in people's lives. For example, one message began:

Good morning, everyone. This is Jim. Yesterday Sue Mason, one of our receptionists, had a successful operation, but they did find some cancer. They think they got most of it out, but she's got to go through some chemotherapy. So let's send our prayers, good energy, and positive thoughts toward Sue.

I hadn't met Sue, but I sent her some positive thoughts anyway. I felt it couldn't hurt. I still hadn't asked anyone about the messages, partly because it never seemed to be the right time to do so. And partly because it had become a bit of a mystery—something to look forward to each day. It had been a long time since I had some mystery in my life.

When I got home at the end of my first week of work, I reflected on my experiences. I was exhausted but had enjoyed the week. Although it was a little stressful learning all the routines and figuring out my job, I was excited and energized. For the most part, my coworkers were friendly, and my boss seemed nice.

Saturday morning, as I sat alone at the breakfast table drinking a cup of coffee, I felt a little sad. I had seen the twins all of ten minutes earlier in the morning. I had planned on making them a nice breakfast, but

they turned me down. They grabbed their own breakfast, which they quickly gulped down. When I offered
to pour some orange juice, Jen announced, "Mom, we're
not little kids anymore!"—implying that I had offended
her—and headed out the door for a swim meet.

That set the tone for the weekend. I hardly saw
the kids at all the next two days. And when they were
around, they didn't seem interested in talking with
me. I tried to tell Jen about my new job, but she listened politely for only a moment and then excused
herself. When I asked Alex how the week had gone, he
looked up briefly from his computer, said, "Fine," and
resumed what he had been doing. *Ah*, I thought, *they're
moving into the next phase of development—independence.
They don't need me the way they used to. Good thing I took
this job.*

By Sunday night, I was bored and looking forward
to going back to work. I went to bed early and was
wide awake the next morning at 5:30. No point in
trying to go back to sleep. I used to drive Jen and
Alex to swim practice before school. Now that they
were in high school, they car-pooled with older team-
mates. Obviously they didn't care if I made breakfast
for them. What to do? I considered going into work
early. I had been assigned a project. If I did a good
job, it might prove my capabilities. *Why not get at it?*
I thought. I dressed quickly, left a note for Jen and
Alex telling them I had left for work, and arrived there
around 6:30.

It hadn't occurred to me that the building would
be locked. Walking around the side, I tested the doors

and found one unlocked in the back. I entered the quiet building with a bit of trepidation. I hadn't met many of the people who worked there yet, and I didn't want to be arrested for breaking and entering.

The door opened to a hallway. I was immediately drawn to the aroma of freshly brewed coffee coming from a room to my left. I poked my head in and noticed several photocopy machines. To my delight, I found fresh coffee in a coffeemaker on a counter near the entrance to the room. It smelled so wonderful that I walked over and helped myself to a cup. As I was enjoying the first sip, I heard a "humpf" behind me.

Startled, I turned and spilled my coffee. I hadn't noticed a small table almost hidden in the back of the room behind a row of copy machines, nor had I noticed the man sitting at it. But clearly he had noticed me. He sat comfortably with a cup of coffee and appeared to have been watching me for some time.

"Care to join me?" he invited.

Self-consciously, I wiped up the spilled coffee and joined him.

"I'm new here," I explained hesitantly. "I wanted to come in early to get some work done, and this was the only door open."

At first I thought he was a custodian or security guard and worried that I might be in trouble. I was quickly assured that was not the case. He was the kind of person who immediately made you feel at ease. We chatted easily. He was an attentive listener and showed genuine interest in me. Although I'm a private person, I was surprised at how much I opened up with him. I told him about getting married so young, how hard it had been caring for a dying husband and two babies.

"I couldn't imagine what it would be like to lose my beloved wife and raise our kids on my own," he said gently.

"It has been tough," I said. "I put my life on hold to raise my kids, and now they don't seem to need me anymore. Truth be told, this is my first real job. I'm both excited and nervous about it."

It suddenly occurred to me that I was being rude. "Forgive me," I said. "You're such a good listener that I've monopolized the conversation—and I don't even know your name."

"My name is Jim, and I'm the president of the agency," he said with a smile. "I enjoyed meeting you, Ellie, and learning about your life. I'm glad you've joined our company. And now, if you'll excuse me, it's time for me to get to work." He stood up and walked off, leaving me stunned and speechless.

Later that morning, when I listened to my voice mail, I heard the following message:

Good morning, everyone. This is Jim. It's a little after 7:00. I was talking this morning with Ellie, our new associate in the accounting department, and I was reminded of a story I'd like to share with you.

One day an expert in time management was speaking to a group. He pulled out a one-gallon, wide-mouthed jar and set it on the table in front of him. He also produced about a dozen fist-sized rocks and carefully placed them, one at a time, into the jar. When the jar was filled to the top and no more rocks would fit inside, he asked, "Is this jar full?"

Everyone said yes.

He then reached under the table and pulled out a bucket of gravel. He dumped some gravel in and shook the jar, causing pieces of gravel to work themselves down into the spaces between the rocks. He then asked the group once more, "Is the jar full?"

But this time some of the group were not so sure.

"Good," he said as he reached under the table and brought out a bucket of sand and dumped it in the jar. Once more he asked the question, "Is the jar full?"

No one answered.

He then grabbed a pitcher of water and poured it in until the jar was filled to the brim. He looked at the class and asked, "What's the point of this illustration?"

One bright young man said, "The point is, no matter how full your schedule is, if you really think about it, you can always fit more things in it."

"No," the speaker replied with a smile. "That's not the point. That's what most people think. The truth this illustration teaches is that if you don't put the big rocks in first, you'll never get them in at all."

What are the big rocks in your life? Time with your loved ones, your dreams, your health, a worthy cause? Remember to put these in first, or you'll never get them in at all.

So, one part of the mystery was solved. The voice mail messages came from Jim, the company's president. Although I now knew who was leaving the messages, I still didn't know why.

I kept my questions to myself and hurried through another busy day without thinking further about the remaining mystery or the message. Darryl had asked me to create a standardized form for agents to complete in order to be reimbursed for their out-of-pocket expenses. He wanted each type of expense to be coded and categorized so they could be easily input into the accounting records. It was complicated as there were many different types of expenses, and Darryl wanted each type listed separately.

That night as I lay in bed, I thought about what the big rocks were in my life. My children, certainly. And my new job. What else? I drifted off with images of rocks surrounding me—and I was stuffed in a jar with them.

● ● ●

Tuesday, I again awoke at 5:30 and hopped out of bed. This time I knew exactly what I was going to do. The evening before, I had asked Alex and Jen whether they would mind if I left for work before they left for school. As I expected, they said it was fine. So, I arrived at the office at about 6:30. I wondered whether Jim would be there. I tested the back door, and it opened. I walked directly to the supply room, and there he was, sitting quietly at the almost-hidden table. He didn't seem surprised to see me.

"Good morning, Ellie," he said. "You're early again today. Want to tell me more?" he invited with a smile.

"Nope," I replied. "It's your turn. I've got some questions for you." I plunged right in. "Why do you leave a voice mail message every morning? How long have you been doing it? What do you want to accomplish? How do you keep thinking of new things to say? Do you get tired of doing it?"

"Whoa!" Jim responded. "You weren't kidding yesterday when you said you were eager to figure things out quickly."

We both laughed as I poured myself a cup of coffee.

Again, I was amazed how at ease I felt chatting with Jim. Knowing that he was the president of the company should have intimidated me. But he was so real and down-to-earth that I couldn't help liking and feeling comfortable with him.

Smiling, Jim continued, "Those are good questions, but I'm not sure I have all the answers. "I left the first message about a year ago. The husband of one of our employees, Alice, had been rushed to the ICU with a mysterious illness. Turns out it was a life-threatening infection and his prognosis wasn't good. Alice asked me to send my prayers for her husband, which I was more than happy to do. Then I thought, 'Why just me—why not everyone?' The next morning I left a voice mail message for everyone and asked them to send their prayers, good thoughts, and energy to Alice's husband. I had no idea what impact that would have on Alice or the agency. I just thought it was a good thing to do. Alice called me in tears the next day. Her husband had turned a corner and things were looking up. She was crying because she was so touched by the message I had left and all the responses she had gotten as a result. And I got feedback from a lot of people saying how wonderful my message was. I thought, 'I'm onto something here.'

"We had been growing so fast as a company that no one knew the important stuff going on in one another's lives. By leaving that voice mail message company-wide, I was able to help us regain something of a small company feeling."

"So your messages helped keep people connected with each other?" I ventured.

"Yes, I guess you might say that. But I think there's more. I also saw how they created energy and a sense of community," Jim replied thoughtfully. "I feel like these messages are making a difference even though I'm not sure how. I think they're good for the agency and good for me."

"How are the messages good for you?" I asked.

"Well, if I'm going to leave a message every morning, I have to spend some time thinking about what's important. I need to compose my thoughts and focus. I used to jump out of bed in the morning and hit the pavement running. Leaving these messages forces me to slow down a bit before I speed up."

"Recently I've asked my assistant to type up my messages and post them online. Occasionally an employee will post a response, although it's all quite informal."

"So if I miss a day, I can get a written version? That's great," I said, "because a couple of times I wanted to review them. But what I like the best is hearing your messages in your voice. It's more powerful."

"That's what I think, too," Jim replied. "Ellie, your questions and views are refreshing. And I would like to talk with you more. But now it's time for me to get going." I looked at my watch and was amazed! I couldn't believe how quickly the time had flown by.

I went to my cubicle and began working. Darryl had asked me to create another standardized form for agents to complete while they were traveling. This form was for their credit card charges so the charges could be entered in the accounting system and coded quickly. Later that morning when I checked my voice mail, there it was—Jim's message for the day. It began:

 Good morning, everyone. This is Jim.

> *Leaving you these morning messages has really helped me because so often I'm tempted to race out of bed, jump into my task-oriented self, get on the phone, start writing and tackling tasks. When I do that, suddenly my day takes off, and it's out of my control. Leaving these messages forces me to think about what's important before I jump into my day.*

I was fascinated by this message. I had met with Jim on two occasions, and a part of both conversations were woven into his morning messages.

What Is Vision, Anyway?

Wednesday, I arrived precisely at 6:30 A.M. There was Jim at the back table. He immediately began talking as though yesterday's conversation had just occurred.

"I knew I was onto something by the tremendous response I got from my first voice mail message. Let me tell you a bit about the history of our company so you'll understand what I was looking for.

"My father was an amazing man. He started this agency from nothing—sheer guts, loans, and a belief in people. Everyone adored Dad—the employees, our customers—especially the widows. He had a tremendous effect on people and made them feel important. There was a real family feeling and joy in the agency. It sparkled."

"It sounds like your dad was a very special person," I said.

"He certainly was," said Jim. "When my father was president, there was a tremendous amount of energy, excitement, and passion. Everyone knew they were making a difference, building a company that provided a real service to the community."

"And now?" I asked.

"It's not the same. I was proud to work my way up through the ranks. I took the helm a little over ten years ago when Dad was getting ready to retire. We had grown quite a bit, and I think he was frustrated that he didn't know everybody anymore, including the customers. Unfortunately, I didn't get much of his guidance during the transition, as he died shortly after I took over."

"That's too bad," I said softly.

"Thanks, Ellie. I think I've been an effective manager over the years. I set clear goals and wander around catching people doing things right, and if they're off base, I redirect their efforts. I think people respect me and like to work here. But something is missing—that old sparkle that I saw in the company when I was young and my father was inspiring everyone."

"The company seems to be doing well financially," I offered.

"That's true, but I haven't had the impact I know I can have. I guess I've been hoping that my morning messages might regenerate some of the magic and energy we used to have."

I thought a moment. "So, you're the president of a successful, respected agency. The company is financially sound, but the sparkle isn't there. You feel like you are a good manager, but there must be something more, and you don't know what it is."

"That about sums it up," he replied.

"It also sounds like it's not that exciting or fulfilling for you, either," I said.

Jim laughed heartily. "Ellie, I'll be honest with you. You're absolutely right. I like it here, but I'm not excited to be here."

Glancing at his watch, he noted, "I've got to get to a meeting now." As he headed for the door he paused a moment, then turned to me. "It seems there's more to be said. How about continuing our discussion tomorrow morning?"

"Sounds great," I said.

It was a busy day at work as quarterly taxes, one of my key responsibilities, were due in two weeks. But during my few free moments I found myself reflecting on what Jim had told me. It felt great to be able to exercise my mind and think about the business world again after all these years.

• • •

Early Thursday morning as we sat drinking coffee, I said to Jim, "Yesterday you said that when your dad was in charge, everything was full steam ahead. I've been thinking about that phrase and wondering what it means to you."

"That was a term used during the day of the steamships. It meant they were fully powered and moving ahead full force."

"Wasn't it also a phrase used in a war? I remember, 'Damn the torpedoes. Full steam ahead,'" I continued.

Jim smiled. "Now you've hooked me. I'm a bit of a history buff. That was Admiral Farragut in the Civil

War. It might have been 'full steam ahead' or 'full speed ahead,' but you're right. He did say 'damn the torpedoes,' refusing to consider retreat in spite of the mines ahead. Why do you ask?"

"I was wondering if *full steam ahead* also means being reckless and blindly moving ahead in the face of danger."

"No, I think it's the opposite. It means being so clear about your purpose, so committed to it, and so sure about your ability to accomplish it that you move ahead decisively despite any obstacles."

Jim paused a second and added, "That's exactly how our agency was when my father was alive."

"Jim, would you tell me more about what your father did to make that happen?" I asked.

"That's easy. Dad had a vision of what he wanted this place to be, and everyone here shared it. He wanted to create an insurance agency that customers loved. He did that by creating an agency that loved customers. They didn't treat people as another potential policy, but as folks who needed help, support, and personal problem solving about their financial futures. Everyone in the agency knew their job was to make a difference for our customers. Oh, and by the way, they made a lot of money."

Jim laughed and continued, "At times it seemed that Dad was like a third-grade teacher. He repeated the message over and over and over again, 'Take care of the customer, and the rest will take care of itself.' And when they got it right, something magical happened—a tremendous amount of energy, excitement, and passion was released. Because people knew they shared the same vision, they trusted and respected each other. There was room for creativity when it came to solving problems. People could make their contributions in their own way, and differences were respected because everyone knew they were in the same boat together, all part of a larger whole."

"It sounds powerful," I mused.

"It was," Jim replied. "I know, because I've experienced it. We were all heading in the same direction, full steam ahead."

"So, *full steam ahead* really does describe the power of vision!"

Jim smiled and then grew serious. "The problem is, times have changed. We're bigger, and the industry has changed. It's more complicated with legislation and red tape, and there are so many new people here who didn't know Dad or grow up in the industry. Even if Dad were here today, I don't know if his vision would provide the guidance needed. Our conversation has made me realize the importance of creating a shared vision. That's the key to the sparkle that's missing. I see now that I had focused only on establishing a well-run, operationally solid, financially sound company. But being a good manager is not enough. Leadership is about going somewhere. I need to get clear about where I want to take the agency."

"That sounds great, Jim!" As the words left my mouth, another question popped up. "But if you don't have a vision, how do you get one? What is it that makes a vision?"

Jim laughed. "That's the question, Ellie. My dad had an intuitive sense of where he wanted to take the agency, and his charismatic personality drew people in. The only problem is that he was the glue. Without him, the sparkle has faded."

"It seems to me that charisma shouldn't have to be a prerequisite for having a vision. There must be another way to create a vision," I mused.

"I like your candor, your fresh perspective, and the way your mind works," Jim said. "You push me to think in ways I don't normally think."

Jim then made an offer that changed my life.

"Ellie, if you're interested, I'd like to talk with you some more and figure out together what vision really is."

Without a moment's hesitation, I replied, "How should we start?"

"I think we should start by taking it apart. Let's see if we can identify the key elements of a vision—one that is compelling, that provides direction and inspires people to participate."

"And when do we start?"

Jim replied, "I come in early almost every morning. I like to sit here quietly before the rush of the day begins. It's a great time for thinking and reflection. I chose this place because it's a storage supply room in the back of the building where people are not likely to notice me. No one's discovered my secret morning hideout until now. How about using this time to think about vision?"

"Sounds good to me. Same time, same place tomorrow."

• • •

Full steam ahead intrigued me. That night I did some research to see what I could find out about steam engines. I learned that the steam engine was without doubt one of the most influential inventions in the development of industry and civilization. In fact, the development of the steam engine made modern industry possible. Until then, people had to rely on their own muscles, the wind, or animals such as horses for power. One steam engine could do the work of hundreds of horses. It could supply all the power needed to run the machines in a factory. A steam locomotive could haul thousands of tons of freight. Steamships provided fast, dependable transportation. *Full steam ahead* certainly did describe the transformative power unleashed by vision.

I couldn't wait to share my discovery with Jim in the morning.

Element 1:
Significant Purpose

"That's great, Ellie," Jim said the next morning when I told him what I had learned. "The advent of the steam engine introduced a strong source of energy and power and created a transformation. Equating the power of vision with the power of the steam engine makes sense.

"Now I've got something to share with you," he continued. "Remember when you pressed me to say what *full steam ahead* really means?"

"Yes. You said it means being fully powered, knowing where you're going, and moving ahead full force."

"That's right. I also said it means being so clear about your purpose, so committed to it, and so sure about your ability to accomplish it that you move ahead decisively despite any obstacles."

"I remember," I said with a smile.

"Well, I woke up with an 'aha.' I realized that *purpose* is an important part of vision. Dad *was* passionate about our purpose, and he made sure that everyone in the agency understood and supported it. I think it was one of the secrets to Dad's vision."

"Tell me more," I invited.

"By *purpose*, I mean understanding what we are here for, why we exist. Purpose means understanding what business we are *really* in so that we all can focus our efforts in support of that purpose."

Jim continued, "What business do you think we are *really* in, Ellie?"

"That's easy," I replied. "The insurance business."

Jim paused a moment and said, "That's what I thought until this morning when I asked myself, *What do people really want when they purchase insurance*? Insurance policies are our products and services. Why do people purchase those products and services? What do they really want from us?"

"Okay, are we in the customer service business?" I asked, taking a random guess.

Jim laughed and prompted, "Ellie, have you made any purchases lately?"

"Hardly," I laughed. "No money. Oh, wait. I did buy a new mattress last year. But what's that got to do with anything?"

"Why did you buy it?"

I thought about it for a moment. I had been waking with a backache frequently. A chiropractor had suggested that I replace the twenty-year-old mattress that had been a hand-me-down from Doug's parents. So that's why I'd bought a new mattress. I reflected further. Why had I bought that particular mattress? What had I been looking for in a mattress? Actually,

I'd spent a great deal of time testing several different mattresses in the store. I had tried a variety of sleeping positions. I'd been looking for a comfortable mattress that would hold its shape over the years so I could get a good night's rest. Then I got what Jim was driving at.

"I wanted to buy a good night's rest."

Jim's face lit up. "Exactly! So that's the business mattress sellers are *really* in—a good night's rest. Now, what business are we *really* in here?"

Why do people buy insurance? I thought about my own situation. I had health insurance and car insurance. I was certainly grateful for Doug's life insurance policy. What had I really wanted when I'd purchased those policies? I'd wanted to feel financially secure in case something bad happened.

"I get it! People who buy insurance want peace of mind for the future. They want financial security for possible worst-case scenarios such as serious illnesses, accidents, or death."

Jim nodded. "That's what I think, too. They want financial peace of mind for the future that doesn't diminish their peace of mind in the present by costing more than they can afford. And they want peace of mind in knowing they'll get the help they need if they need to place a claim.

"Our agents know what kinds of questions to ask to find out exactly what peace of mind and security mean to each of our customers. There are so many options today, it can be overwhelming. Our agents' job is to decipher, decode, and demystify all this to help our customers choose the best products and services to fit their individual needs. And our customer service reps provide security when our customers have claims issues, need answers to questions about benefits, or need comparative pricing.

"Understanding what business we're really in is essential for everyone in our agency. It affects what products and services we provide, how we market them, and even how our receptionist answers the phone.

"My father understood that looking at what we provide from the viewpoint of the customer would give us a deeper sense of purpose. That's probably why he continually emphasized the importance of customer relationships. We aren't just selling insurance; we are serving our customers by providing them with security and peace of mind."

I nodded. "That's really powerful. So, you think *purpose* is an important part of a vision?"

"I do," Jim replied. "I think it's a key element."

"What about mission?" I asked. "I see all these statements on walls in places like supermarkets and fast-food restaurants. Come to think of it, I saw one on the wall in the dry cleaner's. Some have titles like 'Our Mission.' Is that the same as purpose?"

"Sometimes," Jim replied. "No doubt, good mission statements include a clear statement of purpose. Unfortunately, I think the term *mission* is so overused and has so many different meanings that it's become confusing, so I think it's simpler to use the term *purpose*. But I don't think it matters what you call it as long as it explains 'Why do we exist?' and 'What business are we really in?'"

• • •

Later that morning I listened to Jim's morning voice mail message. I wasn't at all surprised by what I heard.

 Good morning, everyone. This is Jim. I want to congratulate everyone on our outstanding first quarter.

One of the ways we continue to pull off this team effort is by remembering what business we're really in. We provide insurance products. But this isn't what our customers really want. No one would voluntarily spend their money on insurance unless they could look in a crystal ball and know for sure they'd need it. But they do want to spend their money on peace of mind—peace-of-mind for the future without diminishing their peace of mind in the present. So I think we're in the financial peace of mind business. What do you think? If that's what business we're in, we need to be sure that our customers are offered a package that meets their particular needs, within their own budgets.

How do we support a purpose like creating peace of mind? It might seem easier for those of you who have direct contact with our customers. But I challenge each of us to think about how we could support a peace-of-mind purpose in our own way, no matter what our role is here in the agency. Why would that be important? Because if the business we're in from our customers' point of view is peace of mind, we must remember why we exist and stay focused on that purpose. Then we'll be able to keep up the good work. Let's begin a dialogue about our purpose. Have a great weekend, everyone!

• • •

Over the weekend I thought about purpose. Once I started looking, I began seeing purpose everywhere. I watched the local Friday night news and realized that one purpose of the local network news is to provide entertainment. The attractive news anchors, weather reporter, and sportscaster chatted easily with each other. They all seemed like friends and engaged in humor-filled banter. They offered an enjoyable way to catch up on the news of my city and region.

I switched to CNN. While CNN's newscasters also engaged in a bit of humor-filled banter, their focus appeared to be providing information on breaking stories around the nation and world. I wanted to learn more about CNN's purpose, so I went to its website and learned that CNN provides twenty-four-hour in-depth coverage of live and breaking national and global news as it unfolds. CNN's viewers are typically busy people who want news on demand. CNN and the local network evening news have two very different purposes for two very different types of customer needs.

I then began an Internet search that took me through the weekend. Even though Jim felt it was simpler to use the term *purpose*, I searched for both "company purpose statements" and "company mission statements" because as he also had suggested, a good mission statement would include a clear purpose statement. I spent hours looking at them.

Some of the statements were inspiring and focusing statements that explained why the company existed and what need it served from the customers' viewpoint. Many sounded so bland that I couldn't imagine they would inspire anyone. Some might be inspiring but were so general I couldn't imagine they would provide any focus or direction. One such statement was "Our mission is to walk our talk."

One well-known company's mission was "to exceed the expectations of our customers. We will accomplish this by committing to our shared values and achieving the highest levels of customer satisfaction." *What business are they really in? What need do they fulfill from their customers' point of view? What purpose do they serve?* I had no idea.

I found a mission statement for a Fortune 500 company that said, "To combine aggressive strategic marketing with quality products and services at competitive prices to provide the best value for consumers." I had no idea what that meant or how their purpose was different from any other company. It sounded like jargon to me.

It occurred to me that there are a lot of mission statements and lots of opinions on how to write them, but not much agreement or consistency on what actually makes a mission statement work in terms of defining the purpose of a business.

I next did a search for company purpose statements, which yielded the same results. Most didn't explain why the companies existed or what business they were in from their customers' viewpoint, as Jim had suggested they might.

I did find a clear and inspiring statement from the Yarmouth Fire Department: "We will do our best to protect people and property in Yarmouth from harm, to improve their safety, to educate the public to prevent emergencies and provide quick and effective responses." I thought, *This is what I, from a customer's viewpoint, want from a fire department; they are thinking about their purpose from a results viewpoint, not just a service-provided viewpoint.* I hoped the firefighters in my own city saw their purpose in a similar manner.

In contrast, I read the purpose statement of a police department from another city. It said that their purpose was "to enforce the law." I found myself asking, "To what end?" In other words, *why* did they provide that service—to "enforce the law"? I thought a better statement would be "to defend citizens' constitutional rights and protect people from harm." That would be a much more compelling and focusing purpose, in my opinion.

I read that when Walt Disney started his theme parks, he declared they were in the "happiness business." I liked that.

On Google's website, I found one of the statements I liked best: "To organize the world's information and make it universally accessible and useful." It was short, clear, and specific.

It was becoming obvious to me that a good purpose statement needed to explain "why," and it needed to "serve a greater good."

Later in the weekend, I did a search of newspaper and magazine articles. I found an interesting article in the *New York Times*. Harvey Mackay, chairman of Mackay Envelope Company in Minneapolis and author of *Swim with the Sharks without Being Eaten Alive*, had adopted the statement "to be in business forever." That didn't seem to meet the criteria of a good statement—it was fuzzy and not inspiring or focusing. But as I read on, I realized that the statement actually had meaning to the employees of Mackay Envelope. According to Mackay, "The emphasis on staying in business forever tells employees to focus on the long term and not to push too hard a bargain with customers and suppliers because customers might go to other companies and suppliers might give their best new technologies to competitors." This statement didn't clarify what business Mackay Envelope was in, but it did convey more meaning than I had originally thought.

I began to realize that the most important thing was the *meaning* of the statement—and not simply what it said. The best words in the world would be meaningless if they meant nothing to the people in the organization. I realized having a mission statement didn't necessarily create focus and inspiration. On the other hand, a good statement of purpose that really held meaning for the people in the company could have a lot of power.

• • •

I was absorbed all weekend by my investigations of purpose and mission, and I could hardly wait to discuss it with Jim. Monday, promptly at 6:30 A.M., I tested the back door of the office building and let myself in.

Jim was sitting at the table drinking coffee. "How was your weekend?" he asked.

I told him all about my weekend search.

"I've come to the conclusion that most purpose and mission statements usually just describe the products and services the company provides at best and at worst are a meaningless collection of platitudes."

Jim commented, "No wonder so many people see this as a useless activity."

"Yes, most statements looked like they were written for marketing to attract customers, rather than to be useful for employees."

We decided to create a list of the criteria for a significant purpose statement. Together, we came up with this list, which Jim wrote on a note card and tacked on the wall:

PURPOSE

- Purpose is your organization's reason for existence.

- It answers the question "Why?" rather than just explaining what you do.

- It clarifies—from your customers' viewpoint— what business you are *really* in.

- Great organizations have a deep and noble sense of purpose—a *significant* purpose—that inspires excitement and commitment.

- The words themselves are not as important as their meaning to the people.

"I think it's a good idea to title our card *purpose* and not *mission*," I said. "I agree with you, Jim, that in order for a mission statement to be effective, it needs to include a statement of clear purpose. While a good mission statement might also include a description of how the people in a company deliver on the purpose, what their products and services are, and how they support the purpose, a mission statement that only describes what they provide or how they provide it—without explaining purpose—comes off as unfocused, unmotivating, and meaningless."

As we readied to leave the room, I said to Jim, "I'm still curious about the purpose of your daily voice mail messages. When I asked you last week, it seemed you weren't clear. You felt leaving them was important, but you didn't know why."

"That's a fair question, Ellie. I'm leaving for an association conference later this morning and will be gone the rest of the week. I'll think about it while I'm gone. How's that?"

"Great!" I replied. "Have a good trip."

Gone for the rest of the week? I was struck by how much I would miss our morning time together and how important our friendship was becoming to me.

• • •

I spent the rest of the week focused on Darryl's project and preparing the quarterly taxes. The agents didn't seem to appreciate the forms Darryl had asked me to create. When I tried to make appointments with them to explain how to use them, most said they were too busy to meet with me. I did finally meet with a couple of agents who were polite but disinterested. I was beginning to pick up tension between Darryl and the agents. In the hallway I had overheard some of the agents complaining about Darryl being a pain in the neck. Darryl wasn't exactly Mr. Personality, but he had struck me as a conscientious person who was sincere about doing his job accurately and efficiently.

When I asked Darryl why he wanted to create these forms, he explained that the company had grown so much that it was difficult to keep track of expenditures. The agents didn't turn in their receipts in a timely manner, which made it difficult for him to generate his reports on time because he had to spend too much time chasing people down. He and Marsha had decided that the forms would save them time tracking down the information they needed. In so many words, Darryl basically said the agents were disorganized and financially irresponsible. I had a gut feeling the forms were not going to solve any problems. But being the new kid on the block, I didn't say anything.

• • •

That evening I thought about the accounting department from the perspective of what Jim and I had learned. My first day on the job, Marsha had explained to me that the accounting department was responsible for receipt of money, paying bills, payroll, recording and tracking assets and inventory, financial reporting, and compiling and filing taxes. This was a list of the activities and services, but it was not a purpose, at least not as Jim and I had defined purpose. I wondered if it would help the accounting department if its purpose were clearly defined. It wasn't just Darryl who was at odds with the agents. I was picking up joking comments about the agents by others in the accounting department, and they left me feeling uneasy. I had a one-on-one meeting scheduled for later in the week with Marsha. I considered whether I might mention any of this to her but decided in the meantime to keep my head down and get my work done.

• • •

Wednesday morning Marsha welcomed me into her office.

"How are you doing, Ellie?" she began. "Now that you've been here a couple of weeks, I thought it would be a good time for a general check-in to see how things are going for you."

I told her how glad I was to be there and how much I was enjoying my new job, the work, and the people. We chatted for a bit about the projects I had been working on and what I was learning. She said she had gotten good reports on how quickly I was picking things up and was going to increase my responsibilities sooner than she'd originally planned. She asked if I had any questions or concerns, so I asked her to tell me more about the overall purpose of the accounting department.

Marsha went to her bookcase and took out what looked like a college textbook. She thumbed through the table of contents, turned to a page, and smiled. She read, "The role of the accounting department is to track and maintain records of all revenue and expenditures in order to control and account for funds." She seemed pleased that she had been able to answer my question quickly. So I thanked her for the explanation and excused myself.

I was perplexed. Did that really explain the department's purpose? What business were we *really* in—from our customers' perspective? Who were our customers, anyway? After talking with others in the accounting department, I was coming to the conclusion that the department had a generally held belief that they—the accounting department—were the customers. They didn't use that language, but it was clear that they believed the primary purpose of their job was to collect and organize financial information, and it was everyone else's job to provide the information they requested in a timely manner.

Chatting with a couple of my new friends in the accounting department at lunch on Thursday, I mentioned that the agents weren't using the new forms Darryl and I had created. They laughed and explained that the agents were "disorganized prima donnas" who expected everyone else to clean up after them. They said, "Just get used to it, Ellie. It's the way things are. Darryl is wasting his time and yours."

On Friday morning, something very interesting occurred. Darryl quit. Actually, we weren't sure that he had really quit, but he had stormed out of the office and hadn't come back after lunch. I wasn't there when it happened, but I heard there was a big blow up between him and one of the agents. There was yelling, name-calling, and then Darryl stormed out. Everyone was quite abuzz. It was totally out of character for Darryl, who was generally a contained, nonexpressive person. The argument was with Eugene, one of the agents I hadn't met but who had a reputation for being a fun-loving guy who liked to joke around. Apparently he had made a disparaging remark about what Darryl could do with his forms.

I spent the afternoon finishing up not only my work but also some of Darryl's. I knew he had an important report due next week. In hopes that he hadn't really quit and would be back on Monday, I thought I might be able to help him out by inputting the data for his report. I had to track down some of the information but was able to collect most of it.

As I finished up, I looked at the time and realized it was later than usual. The office was mostly empty, but the light was on in Marsha's office and her door was open. As I passed by on my way out, she noticed me and invited me in.

"Great way to start a new job, Ellie," she remarked glumly. "You're not seeing the best of who we are."

"Frankly, I'm surprised." I replied. "Darryl doesn't seem like the kind of person to walk out on a job."

"He's not." Marsha said. "I'm very surprised also. Darryl and Eugene have both been with us for years, and nothing like this has happened before. They weren't friends, but they've always been cordial."

She was so open and approachable that I felt it would be okay to share what was on my mind.

"Do you mind if I share some observations?" I asked. "Being the new kid on the block and all, I might be overstepping my bounds. But sometimes when you're new you see things from a perspective that others who are caught in the middle of things can't see."

Marsha had the same easygoing manner as Jim. "Shoot," she said.

"I'm wondering if the issue is not a personality clash between Darryl and Eugene but something else."

"What else do you think it could it be?" Marsha asked, her attention suddenly attuned.

"Jim and I have had some conversations about purpose—what business you are in."

"Yes, he's told me a bit and that he has a lot of respect for your intelligence and intuition. And I respect his intuition about people. So, I'm open to hearing your thoughts."

"I'm wondering if the argument was provoked because of a difference in how the agents see the purpose of the accounting department."

"Okay. Tell me more."

I shared with Marsha what Jim and I had learned about purpose. I told her I hadn't been able to figure out what the purpose of the accounting department was, from the viewpoint of the customers, because I wasn't sure who the customers were. When I had conversations with the agents, they jokingly referred to the accounting department as the "numbers police" because we were always requesting data, making sure it's correct and on time.

Marsha let out a sigh. "So, you're saying that we need to be clear about why we are collecting financial information and who needs to use that information."

"Right," I said. "What business is our accounting department really in—and who are our customers?"

Marsha's eyes twinkled. "And you think if we could communicate our purpose clearly and share it with other departments, we might be able to work collaboratively as business partners rather than feeling like we're on competing teams."

"Yes, I do, Marsha. It's easier to blame conflict on personality issues. But my children are on a great swim team, and I've seen that kids with very different personalities get along fine when they are committed to the same team."

"And a first step to being on the same team is to understand and agree on how we each contribute to the team," Marsha mused.

I was impressed with how quickly Marsha put things together and even took them a step further.

• • •

Three weeks had flown by and I had hardly seen my children, so I decided to spend the weekend reconnecting with them. But it seemed they had other ideas. Every time I suggested we do something together, they had conflicting plans.

So I spent much of the weekend fixing things up—shopping, doing laundry, and catching up on my to-do list. By Sunday night I had a well-stocked refrigerator, a clean house, and a strong desire to get back to work.

• • •

On Monday morning I was practically accosted by Marsha as I entered the building. She invited me directly to her office.

"Ellie, I had a very busy weekend, in part because of you. I had a long talk with Darryl on Saturday. The good news is he's staying with the company. I wasn't going to let him go—he's too valuable. He was pretty frustrated, and I had to talk with him for a long time. The conversation you and I had on Friday helped me get Darryl to look at the situation from a wider perspective. I promised him that things will be different."

"Glad to hear he's back," I said.

"We have a lot of work to do," Marsha replied. "I'm calling a department meeting for Wednesday morning to get started."

Heading to my desk, I stopped by Darryl's cubicle to say hello. He was appreciative of the work I had done for him Friday afternoon. He had gotten an idea for a new form that he wanted me to start working on.

It was late morning by the time I was able to play Jim's morning message. It confirmed that he had spent time on his trip considering the question I had been asking him: why he was leaving these voice mail messages.

Good morning, everyone. This is Jim. I'd like to explain some of the reasons I've been leaving these messages.

The first one is that I want to remind people to stay in the present and enjoy life. And I want us to keep perspective—to remember to get our egos out of the way and not think that we're the centers of the universe. I guess that's been a constant theme.

Second, I want to help maintain our sense of community as we grow, so that we can harness our collective energy for the benefit of us all. And, I want to catch people doing things right and acknowledge their contributions. I think it's really great that so many of you send messages back to me. And I'm glad I've had an opportunity to forward so many of your views back to everyone.

Third, I want to share myself, my life as a person, what I am doing, what and who touches me, my struggles and joys, and what I'm learning.

Fourth, I want to help determine our purpose—what business we're really in. This is very important as we continue to grow. We need to stay focused on why we exist.

Have a great day!

Later that day I passed Jim in the hallway. We chatted briefly about his trip and he asked if I was going to come in early this week to continue our discussions. I agreed, of course.

• • •

Early the next morning, sitting at our small table tucked behind the copy machines, Jim told me how helpful it was to get clear about the purpose of his morning messages. We agreed that clarifying purpose would also be helpful for teams.

Marsha had told Jim about the events on Friday and that she was going to hold a team meeting to define the purpose of the accounting department. Jim said he had told Marsha that he would discuss any thoughts he had about what was happening in accounting directly with her, and he had also reassured her that we weren't discussing anything confidential— our conversations were strictly of a philosophical nature. I was pleased to know that Marsha was supportive of our morning conversations.

Wednesday the accounting department meeting was scheduled to start first thing. *This will be interesting* I thought. *I'll get a chance to see how the power of purpose makes a difference.*

Jim's morning message set the tone for the day.

Good morning, everyone. This is Jim. I'd like to tell you a story this morning that illustrates the power of understanding the purpose of your work. Three workers were busy constructing a building when an observer approached. The first worker was dirty, sweaty, and had an unhappy expression on his face. The observer asked the first worker, "What are you doing?" The worker replied, "I'm laying bricks." The second worker also was dirty, sweaty, and had an unhappy expression on his face. The observer asked the second worker, "What are you doing?" The second worker replied, "I'm making $20 an hour." The third worker was dirty and sweaty but had a beautiful and inspired expression. He worked as hard as the other two, but work seemed to come more effortlessly for him. The observer asked the third worker, "What are you doing?" And he replied, "I'm building a cathedral." I encourage you to look at your work from the perspective of its purpose, not just the activities you are doing.

Marsha opened the meeting by presenting the criteria that Jim and I had developed that defined purpose. We began the meeting with a robust discussion on what business we were really in. Marsha summed it up:

"So often we see ourselves, and are seen by others, as number crunchers rather than business partners. But we need to change that. We need to help our business partners make good business decisions by supplying the accurate and timely information they need. This means we shouldn't just be collecting data and completing forms. We need to be proactive in getting the right information to the right people at the right time. And this means understanding what information people need and when they need it.

We then created the following statement of purpose:

> The accounting department is in the internal financial peace-of-mind business by getting the right financial information to the right people at the right time.
>
> We provide accurate, timely information and advice to guide leaders in wise financial decision making, to develop and maintain effective payroll and accounting systems, and to protect the agency by ensuring compliance with all legal reporting requirements.

We decided the next step would be to each test our purpose statement and hopes with our various customers—the departments we were serving according to our purpose statement—to see if it all made sense.

I was impressed by how much the power of purpose had energized the group. The lively discussions had been an important part of creating that energy. Interestingly, the normally quiet Darryl was one of the most active participants. If everyone had just been handed a typed document from Marsha, I doubted that it would have had much impact at all. As it was, we all left the meeting enthusiastic and focused.

Element 2:
Picture of the Future

The following day I met with Jim bright and early.

"Having a purpose really does make a vision come alive," I said, reflecting on my experience with the accounting department clarifying our purpose. "But it seems to me there's more to vision than purpose. A purpose explains who you are and why you exist, but it doesn't explain where you're going."

"Yes," Jim replied. "A clear vision has to talk about going somewhere."

"What about the Apollo Moon Project?" I wondered. "Some people use it as an example of a vision."

"You mean to put a man on the moon by the end of the 1960s? That was a real statement of a destination," said Jim.

"Yes. Alex is studying this in school right now. He told me that when John F. Kennedy initiated that project, the technology to achieve it did not even exist! NASA overcame what seemed like insurmountable obstacles to achieve that spectacular result."

"I bet there isn't a person who was alive at that time who doesn't remember what he or she was doing the day of the first moon landing," Jim remarked.

"I think what made it powerful was the picture. It was a clear picture of the future that you could imagine happening."

"You're right!" Jim exclaimed. "A picture of the future shows where you're going.

"Here's another example of the power of creating a picture of what you want to achieve," he continued excitedly. "In the 1976 Olympics, the Soviet athletes walked away with almost all the gold medals. They won more gold than any other country, even in events they weren't expected to win. Everyone was absolutely stunned. Some people questioned whether the athletes had been on some kind of drugs. But that wasn't the case. The key to their success was that their sports training had involved a technique called mental rehearsal, where the athletes visualized their performance during the competition. Today this technique is commonly used in sports training. At that time, it was very new, and the results were remarkable.

"My daughter Kristen said that she used the technique of visualizing when she was learning to ski moguls—the bumpy hills on a steep slope. She told me that she had taken several lessons on how to ski the bumps but still didn't have much confidence and felt awkward. One day as she stood at the top of a particularly bumpy run, she watched one of the skiers go down quite gracefully. In fact, there was such grace and rhythm it looked as though the skier were

dancing. Kristen then imagined herself skiing with
the same kind of rhythm. She actually saw it in her
mind. Guess what happened next? She did it. She
'danced' down the slope. Since then, Kristen has used
visualization techniques in a variety of situations. She
told me that many sports trainers have gone beyond
the technique of mental rehearsal to simply visualizing
the end result. In other words, instead of having the
athletes mentally practice the gymnastics routine, the
dives, or the ski run, they visualize themselves standing on the podium receiving the gold medal. Think
of that!"

A picture of the end result!

I recalled that when I was investigating purpose,
I found a statement by CNN that its vision was to be
"viewed by every nation on the planet, in English, and
in the language of that region." This certainly was
a clear picture of the end result—it was a picture of
something happening in the future. When I closed
my eyes, I could actually see it. Like Steve Jobs's vision
of a computer on every desk. It was a crisp picture, not
some vague concept such as to be "Number One" or
"The Provider of Choice." Those statements provided
no clarity on destination or direction.

This conversation reminded me of the weight I had
gained after the twins were born. I never lost all the
pregnancy weight; then with caring for two infants
while my husband was dying, I gained more weight.
By the time the twins were four years old, I was almost twenty pounds overweight. I wasn't under stress

anymore—in fact, my life had stabilized—but I just couldn't lose the weight. I tried several diets without success. I would eat what felt like mouse-sized rations and generally felt deprived as I chomped on celery while the children ate ice cream for dessert. I finally gave up. I decided that I'd rather be fat and happy than starving and miserable—except I wasn't really happy with the way I looked. So I was stuck.

Then I found something that actually worked. I pulled my favorite blue jeans out of the drawer, the ones that didn't fit anymore, and hung them up in my bedroom. Each evening before I went to sleep I looked at them and imagined myself wearing them. I visualized how I would look in them. The next morning, I'd do the same thing. It was energizing and encouraging. I started the diet again, but this time with my energy focused on the picture of how I wanted to look, not on the ice cream I was missing out on. It made a huge difference! I lost the weight and never gained it back.

Instead of focusing on what I was giving up, I focused on the picture of what I wanted to create—to look good in my jeans.

I told this story to Jim. We agreed that we had uncovered an important principle:

> *The power of a picture works when you*
> *focus on what you want to create,*
> *not what you want to get rid of.*

In other words: we need to be *proactive*, not *reactive*.

I left work that evening intrigued by the power of picture. I had always been deeply moved by the vision

articulated by Martin Luther King, Jr. I had a copy
of his "I Have a Dream" speech at home. I got it out,
read it, and was struck by the powerful pictures he
created:

> I have a dream that one day on the red hills of
> Georgia *the sons of former slaves and the sons of for-*
> *mer slave owners will be able to sit down together* at the
> table of brotherhood. . . . I have a dream that *my*
> *four little children will one day live in a nation where*
> *they will not be judged by the color of their skin* but by
> the content of their character. . . . I have a dream
> that one day the state of Alabama . . . will be trans-
> formed into a situation where *little black boys and*
> *girls will be able to join hands with little white boys*
> *and girls and walk together as sisters and brothers.* . . .
> We will be able to speed up the day when all
> of God's children, black men and white men,
> Jews and Gentiles, Protestants and Catholics,
> will be able to *join hands and sing* in the words
> of that old Negro Spiritual, Free at last! Free
> at Last! Thank God almighty, we are free
> at last!

These certainly were vivid pictures—if you closed
your eyes, you could actually see them happening.
They weren't vague statements about the importance
of freedom and brotherhood, but clear pictures that
demonstrate what it looks like. I concluded that there
was a tremendous amount of power in having a clear
picture of the desired end result.

Another thing that struck me about Dr. King's pictures was that they were pictures *only* of the end result, not the process of achieving it. He had left it up to us to figure out how to achieve the end result. But the pictures he created are enduring and continue to serve as a beacon. I recalled a similar thing when I was reading about Disney. Walt Disney's picture of the future for his theme parks was expressed in the charge he gave every cast member: "Keep the same smile on people's faces when they leave the park as when they entered." And he didn't care whether the guest was at the park two hours or ten hours. He just wanted to keep them smiling. After all, they were in the happiness business. Once again, Disney didn't tell his people how to do it, but he described the end result he wanted.

The next morning I handed Jim a copy of Dr. King's speech and told him about the underlying principle I had uncovered.

> *The power of a picture works when you*
> *focus on the end result,*
> *not the process to achieve it.*

We summarized on a piece of paper what we had uncovered about the second element of vision:

PICTURE OF THE FUTURE

- A picture of the end result, something you can actually see, not vague

- Focus on what you want to create, not what you want to get rid of.

- Focus on the end result, not the process for getting there.

"Jim, what do you think is the picture of the future for our agency?" I wondered.

"It's not so easy to come up with something simple, like a computer on every desk or a man on the moon," Jim replied.

"Try closing your eyes. What do you see?" I asked.

Jim closed his eyes and sat quietly. After a few moments he opened his eyes and smiled at me.

"I saw smiling customers. They were happy because they trusted that everyone in our company had their best interest in mind. The agents took the time to understand what they needed and were competent in finding the best products and services at the best price. Customers trusted that the agents weren't going to oversell them on things they didn't need. And whenever there was a problem, they only needed to make one call—to us."

"That sounds great, Jim," I replied. "Maybe one image might emerge over time, but right now you could focus on seeing the whole picture. Not just for customers but also for employees and maybe the community as well."

"Good idea, Ellie," Jim replied. "We're getting closer, but obviously there's more work to be done. Carolyn and I are taking a long weekend skiing with some college buddies, and I'll have plenty of time to relax and reflect."

"Lucky you," I replied, considering the weekend ahead. "You get to ski. I get to do laundry."

Jim chuckled. "That's the life of a working mom, right? Have a great rest of the day. Let's meet again on Tuesday next week. Maybe we'll have some more ideas."

Element 3:
Clear Values

I wished Jim a safe and fun journey and headed to work. Not only was it Friday, but it was tax day—my final deadline. Quite a busy day. Just before I headed home, I sat down to relax for a moment and played Jim's morning message. As I listened, I discovered the third element of a vision.

Good morning, everyone. This is Jim. I'm looking forward to a fabulous trip this weekend—my annual ski trip with dear friends Carolyn and I have known since college. I so look forward to this time, as it nurtures my values and I always come back refreshed.

I'd like to read you my values:

"I value spiritual peace. I know that I'm living by this value when I experience the presence of that which is greater than myself and feel that unconditional love."

I feel a lot of that during our reunions. I get up early every morning and enter my day slowly, and really get a sense of being at peace.

Then my second value:

"I value joy. I know that I am living by this value anytime I am feeling playful and anytime I wake up feeling grateful for my blessings, the beauty around me, and the people in my life."

Being around old friends is really a joy. We always have a lot of fun. We've known each other before we were anything, and all of us have done quite well. But we all keep each other grounded when we get together because none of us is overly impressed with our accomplishments.

And my third value: "I value health. I know I'm living by this value anytime I treat my body with love and respect."

Just being in the mountains makes it easy to be aware of eating right and exercising. I'm aware that I've gotten out of shape, and I've decided that I'm going to keep up this healthful lifestyle when I get back home.

It was obvious that Jim was clear about his values and that they guided him on a daily basis.

Values! *What does that word really mean? Why are values important? How are they connected to purpose and a picture of the future?*

That night I began to search for the answers to those questions. I started with the definition in Jen's dictionary.

> value: a belief or ideal; the quality of a thing that makes it wanted or desirable; e.g., the value of true friendship.

That's not a very sophisticated definition, I thought.
Then again, values shouldn't be a sophisticated concept.

Yet, it seemed to me that values are more than just
beliefs—they are deeply held. People care passionately
about their values. We all feel good when we act on
our values.

Using that information, I wrote this definition:

> **Values are deeply held beliefs that certain qualities**
> **are desirable. They define what is right or**
> **fundamentally important to each of us.**
> **They provide guidelines for our choices and actions.**

If purpose is important because it explains "why,"
and a picture of the future is important because it
indicates "where," then values are important because
they explain "how." They answer the question "How
will you behave on a day-by-day basis as you fulfill
your purpose and move toward your picture of the
future?"

That was it!

To test my theory, I went back to the Internet to
look at some companies that had a good purpose statement and picture of the future. Did they also have
clear values?

Bingo!

On the same page as Google's mission was its philosophy of "Ten Things," which articulated their values.

When I looked up Disney again, besides declaring
the company was in the happiness business and had a
mission to keep people smiling, the site also listed four
values: Safety, Courtesy, The Show, and Efficiency.

Southwest Airlines was also an example of what I was looking for. Its site said, "We're in the customer service business. We happen to fly airplanes." The desired result they wanted was that "every American has the 'Freedom to Fly'—to be with friends, business associates, or relatives on happy occasions as well as sad ones." And finally, the values that guide its behavior on a daily basis were Safety, a Warrior Spirit, a Servant's Heart, and a Fun-LUVing attitude.

I had recently read an article that featured Harvest Power, a company that was creating renewable energy from organic waste. I was curious to see if it had a clear purpose, picture of the future, and supporting values. I didn't have to search hard—it was right on its website. At the top of the page was its purpose and picture of the future:

> We envision a world where valuable resources are harvested rather than wasted. Our business is to help society live in balance with nature by providing products and services that harness the energy and nutrients of organic materials, creating a path that transforms wastes into valuable resources that enable communities, businesses, and individuals to thrive sustainably.

Their purpose and picture of the future were followed by five values:

> *Safety:* We design, build, and operate our facilities, offer products and services, and conduct all

our activities in ways that are safe and healthy for our employees, neighbors, customers, and the environment.

Ethics and Integrity: In our interactions with others, whether inside or outside the company, we always act with honesty, integrity, and respect. As we do so, we will build and earn the trust and confidence of each other, our business partners, host communities, and investors on which our success depends.

Sustainability: Our focus for our business and for our world is on the long term. Our products, services, and business practices will promote environmental sustainability while building long-term economic sustainability for the company.

Results: Our ability to realize our vision and fulfill our values depends on delivering on-the-ground results. We will set and pursue ambitious goals, measure our success by what is actually achieved, and learn from our failures.

Passion: We believe passionately in our mission and values, and bring energy and enthusiasm to all our endeavors. Our passion inspires others to work with us to achieve our mission.

I thought it was helpful that Harvest Power clearly defined each of its values, rather than just listing the words. It helped me know exactly what the value meant. It made sense to me that safety would be listed near the top of its values since it was in the business of creating a safe environment. And because it had facilities that operated large equipment, the well-being of each employee was guaranteed by this value.

With all of these companies, I noticed three things about their values. First, the values they chose supported their purpose and picture of the future. Second, they only had a few values—usually four to five. Third, the values often appeared to be rank ordered. I did some research and found that most organizations that do have values either have too many values or have not rank ordered them. However, most people cannot focus on more than four or five values that really impact behavior. I also learned that values are most effective when they are rank ordered, so that when value conflicts arise, people know which value they should focus on.

Later in the weekend, I came across an interesting article from the *New York Times* that supported these findings. It was about Johnson & Johnson's values. "This is the glue that holds this corporation together," said Michael J. Carey, vice president of Johnson & Johnson. "The message is the ability to produce business results, not at any cost, but within our value system." The article described how their rank-ordered values guided them through one of their worst crises: the 1982 incident in which cyanide placed into a bottle of Tylenol killed a customer. Since their number one value had to do with the safety and well-being of their patients, the company quickly recalled the product at a cost of $75 million. They paid a tremendous short-term cost. However, the long-term benefit is that the company not only survived a major crisis but emerged even stronger.

I tried to imagine the discussion of the people who participated in that important decision. They didn't have a lot of time to make it. Did anyone suggest just recalling the bottles in the city where the customer died? Did anyone suggest withholding the information? Did anyone suggest trying to find a scapegoat and blame someone else?

The only way they could make a quick and right decision that day was to use their values to guide them. That difficult decision was in the long-term best interest of the company and the public.

I found another article on Johnson & Johnson posted on May 5, 2010, in the online *Daily Finance*. In May 2010, the FDA released a scathing report on J&J for not moving aggressively enough to clean up problems at one of their plants. The article observed, "The J&J name is one of the most respected brand names in the world. And once that brand takes a hit, it can be a long road to recovery. Years ago, J&J set the bar with its stellar handling of the Tylenol tampering incident. And so far they have not mounted an effective response to current manufacturing problems. But if the company doesn't show that it has solved these woes soon, management may find that the J&J halo grows dimmer." I realized that not only are values important for helping a company move "full steam ahead," but

also that not continuing to act on its values can nega-
tively affect its image and profits.

I revisited the website for CNN. What interested
me was that this organization used its values on the
employment opportunities page to attract the kind of
people who would fit its culture:

> We want employees who—above all—have a pas-
> sion for delivering the news in fast, accurate, and
> compelling ways to the global public we serve. We
> are looking for CNN's future: people with fresh
> ideas, innovative viewpoints, a willingness to work
> hard, and a commitment to the highest standards
> of journalism.

Five values jumped out: fast, accurate, innovative, hard
work, and highest standards of journalism.

When reading about these companies' values, I was
struck by how important it is for a company to state
its values clearly so that it can attract employees whose
values are aligned with the company's.

• • •

I couldn't wait for Jim's return to share my discovery.
Bright and early Tuesday morning, I greeted him with
a huge smile.

"Guess what I did while you were hanging out on
the ski slopes?" I teased. "I figured out the third element of a vision."

"Nice to see you, too," he replied with a grin. "So tell me what is it and how you came by this discovery?"

"From you, my friend," I replied. "The clue was in your morning message on Friday. You were talking about your values, and all of a sudden the pieces of the puzzle fit together. The missing piece was values."

Purpose tells why.
Picture of the future tells where.
Values tell how.

I excitedly told Jim all about my weekend investigations and how I had discovered that the companies that had a significant purpose and picture of the future also had clearly articulated values.

"Here's what I found out about values and how they relate to vision," I said, handing him a note card.

VALUES

- Values provide broad guidelines on how you should proceed as you pursue your purpose and picture of the future.

- They answer the questions "What do I want to live by?" and "How?"

- They need to be few in number and rank ordered in importance.

- They need to be clearly described so you know exactly the behaviors that demonstrate that the value is being lived.

- They need to be consistently acted on, or they are only "good intentions."

- People's personal values need to be in line with the values of the organization.

Jim studied the card. "No doubt about it," he said with enthusiasm. "Values are the third key element of vision. Nice job, Ellie." He tacked my note card on the wall next to the cards titled "Purpose" and "Picture of the Future."

"The best companies have values that support their purpose and picture of the future," I said. "That's what it looked like when I did my Internet search. CNN values speed and high standards of journalism because its business is reporting late-breaking news. Disney values Safety, Courtesy, and The Show because of its entertainment parks."

"That makes sense." Jim agreed. "Values are not just soft 'nice-to-haves.' They're vitally important because they guide people's behavior and decisions on a daily basis as they pursue the *what* and *where*."

Jim continued, "I'm curious about your contention that you only need a few values and they should be rank ordered. I've seen plaques in companies with ten or twelve values. It looks like they're for mother, country, apple pie, and everything in between."

"I bet there were no clear priorities, either," I interjected.

"Not that I could see," said Jim.

I told Jim about the newspaper article I had found when investigating the organization's values that described how Johnson & Johnson's leaders used their values to make the right decisions during the Tylenol tampering crisis in the 1980s.

"Their values, which they call their 'Credo,' are listed in order," I said. "Their number one value is

their commitment to their patients—to provide quality, affordable products. Their *last* value is making a
sound profit for the business and a fair return to their
stockholders.

"The article said that the way the leaders made
that decision so quickly was to consult their values,"
I continued. "It's occurred to me that if their values
hadn't been listed in order, they might have made their
decision based on their value of profitability, rather
than concern for the well-being of their customers."

Jim considered what I was saying. "I think you're
right. Kristen's last year in high school we took a family trip to Disney World. While there, I learned that
safety is their number one value, and courtesy is their
number two value. Ideally, they would act on all their
values all the time. But if there was a conflict between
values, they'd know which one to act on."

I thought about that a moment. "So if a *cast member*—Disney's term for employee—was answering a
guest's question in a courteous way and a scream was
heard, that cast member would immediately excuse
himself and head toward the scream, because his number one value just called," I suggested.

Jim laughed. "Well, that would be a specific
example."

"Then you agree with me that it's important
to only have a few values and list them in order of
importance?"

Jim nodded. "That's right."

"What are the values here—for the agency?" I wondered.

Jim wrinkled his brow. "That's a good question, Ellie. I think they were simply understood when we were a smaller company and my father was president. But we've never articulated them. When I think about the understood but not articulated values that are in place at our agency, I immediately think of *integrity* and *relationships*."

"How do those values help fulfill the purpose of the agency?" I asked.

"If we're in a business that builds peace of mind, this means people need to trust us. They can't trust us unless we act ethically and develop positive relationships."

"That's true," I remarked. "So *integrity* and *relationships* are important values because they support the agency's purpose."

"Absolutely. These values should not only guide our behaviors with our customers but also should guide how we behave with each other within the agency."

Jim continued, "I think there's one more value that's important for us—*success*. If we don't deliver on our promises, we won't grow our business."

"Makes sense to me," I remarked. "Do others in the agency agree?"

"Time to find out!" Jim smiled, stood up, and excused himself.

• • •

Later that morning, I was not at all surprised to hear the following voice mail message:

Good morning, everyone. This is Jim. Today I'd like to talk about values.

Just like people, organizations have values— understood norms that guide the organization's behavior on a daily basis. I've been thinking about which values should be guiding us here, and I'd like to test them out. I believe we need values around integrity, relationships, and success, and we need to identify behaviors that demonstrate what these values look like. We need to be sure we're all acting consistently with our values, and we need to help each other do that. So, I'd like to start talking about this. Do you agree that these are our values? And if you do, how do we demonstrate them?

Jim's message reinforced for me how important it is to describe values in terms of examples of specific behaviors that support them. When Jim shared his personal values, he didn't just say that he valued health. He explained what it looks like when he is acting on that value and what he intends to do to support that value. Now, he was inviting people in the agency to help identify what it looks like when they are acting on the company's values.

• • •

During our copy room chat the following morning, I remarked, "Your voice mail message yesterday seemed to have energized things. Everyone at lunch was talking about the agency's values."

"Great. This is a long-overdue conversation. I'm going to push to make them as clear as the examples you found on the Internet."

"You know, Jim, I see how the best companies are clear about their values and use them to guide behaviors and decisions. But why do you think it's so important?"

"I've been thinking about that, too," Jim responded. "Being clear about my personal values has been so effective for me. There's a lot of power in values. I think it's because values tap into people's feelings. People cherish their values and are deeply emotional about them. When they act in support of their values, they are proud of their actions."

"So we might say that values serve as the driving force behind purpose and picture of the future. Values supply the energy and excitement that help people remain committed when the going gets tough," I replied.

"Yes, especially when personal values are consistent with those of the organization. Ensuring emotional commitment is one reason clearly stated values are so important."

I considered this for a moment. "There could be a second reason. I think shared values also help people behave consistently. I'm reminded of the time I hired a company to fertilize our grass and kill the weeds. They came regularly in the summer. I had asked them to call ahead to let me know they were coming so I could close the windows, pick up the kids' toys from the yard, and make arrangements to take them

somewhere else to play. The company was unpredict-
able. Depending on who was doing the work, some
would call ahead and some wouldn't. Some would
even start spraying with toys scattered in the grass. It
seemed like there were no consistent standards for environmental safety, yet that's an important value that
if articulated, would have guided every person who
sprayed our lawn. Not only would they have consistently called first, but they might even have picked up
toys from the lawn if they came and I wasn't home."

We sat quietly for a while, drinking our coffee and
reflecting on the importance of values.

"I love this values stuff," Jim said as we got up to
go back to work. "It really makes a vision come alive."

• • •

I was not at all surprised when, at our next department
meeting, Marsha asked us to revisit our purpose and
identify the values needed to support it. She contended
that our purpose statement—being in the internal
financial peace-of-mind business—also included a picture of the future: "we will get the right information
to the right people at the right time."

In terms of values, we considered accuracy, de-
pendability, teamwork, integrity, timeliness, respect,
safety, creativity, and fun. Marsha insisted that we
could choose no more than five. I voted for "fun," but
it didn't make the list as someone rightly pointed out
that we weren't in the entertainment business. And
Marsha pointed out that I could still live my personal
values as long as they were not in conflict with the

company or department values. I decided that I would definitely find ways to act on the value of having fun, as Darryl and a couple of others who were always so serious looked like they needed to have a little more fun in their lives. Based on our department's purpose and picture of the future, we established the following rank-ordered values:

- Integrity
- Knowledge and Expertise
- Accountability
- Teamwork

We agreed that the next step was to define them clearly so that we would have a common understanding of exactly what they meant in terms of day-to-day behaviors.

It seemed to me that having a purpose, picture of the future, and clearly defined values had established a true vision for our department. I thought Jim would agree.

Vision Defined

At our next meeting, Jim and I reflected on all the things we'd learned about vision. We were feeling pleased with ourselves.

"I think we've finally uncovered the key elements," Jim said.

The three key elements of a compelling vision:
Significant Purpose
A Picture of the Future
Clear Values

"Would it be a compelling vision if it didn't have all three elements?" I wondered.

"I don't think so," Jim replied. "In the example of the Apollo Moon Project, NASA certainly had a clear picture of the end result, even though the process to achieve it was not clear. The picture focused NASA's energy, and its people accomplished amazing results— all because of the powerful picture of the future. But since that time, they have never re-created that energy or momentum. The power ended."

"True," I remarked. "I would have thought they would have landed on Mars by now."

"I think it's because the underlying purpose was never clearly agreed on. Why were we doing it? Were we doing it to win the space race, to begin the Star Wars space defense initiative, or in the spirit of *Star Trek* 'to boldly go where no one has gone before'? And because there was no significant purpose, there was nothing to guide future decisions. NASA has shown neither clear direction nor outstanding performance since."

I considered those thoughts for a moment. "So that means that the Apollo Moon Project was not a vision—it was a goal with a powerful picture of the future."

"Exactly," Jim agreed. "I think a vision is enduring. It continues to provide guidance as goals are achieved. One way to tell the difference between a goal and a vision is to ask, 'What's next?' A vision offers clear direction for future activity and guides the setting of new goals once the current ones have been achieved. Without a vision, once the goal has been achieved, it's all over."

"That's a good way to put it," I said. "Do you think it applies in every situation?"

"Yes, I do. Take your example about losing weight. You had an image of the end result, but once you had achieved your desired weight, your goal was finished. Right?"

I thought about what he was saying. I did think he was right. Looking thin was only a goal, not a vision, even though I had a picture of the end result in my mind. Losing weight could be a step toward achieving something greater, such as a healthy body or a positive self-image, if I had been clear about that.

"I think we should come up with a crisp definition of a vision," I suggested.

This is what we decided:

VISION DEFINED

Vision is knowing where you are, where you are going, and what will guide your journey.

"'Knowing who you are' means being clear about your purpose. 'Where you are going' is the picture of the future. And 'what will guide your journey' is your values."

"I like this definition," Jim remarked. "If you don't know who you are, it really doesn't matter where you're going."

"And if you're going somewhere, you need to be clear about the values that will guide your journey, to help you make the tough decisions when you hit obstacles," I added.

"It's what allows you to go full steam ahead. If you're on a powerful steamship, you can't control the weather. You know your final destination, but you might need to shift course a bit to ride out a bad storm or avoid an iceberg. Your values allow you to shift course in a way that keeps you in sight of your true destination."

Next we created a checklist to use as a test to make sure the vision is indeed a compelling vision.

TEST OF A COMPELLING VISION

- Helps us understand what business we're *really* in

- Provides a picture of the desired future that we can actually see

- Provides guidelines that help us make daily decisions

- Is enduring

- Is about being "great"—not solely about beating the competition

- Is inspiring—not expressed solely in numbers

- Touches the hearts and spirits of everyone

- Helps each person see how he or she can contribute

We decided that if a vision could pass this test, there was a pretty good chance it would provide clear direction and would mobilize people.

We were both quite excited. We believed we were exploring and learning about something really important and powerful. Jim said that it was also fun—working on the pieces of this puzzle together. Together, we were figuring out things that neither of us would have done on our own.

● ● ●

The next morning, Jim's voice mail message reminded me that the importance of creating a vision is not just for organizations but also for us as individuals.

Good morning, everyone. This is Jim.

Last night I was working on something and thinking that we really have a choice, that good leadership and how we are in the world starts on the inside. We have two choices:

1. Whose are we going to be?

2. Who are we going to be?

You might say it sounds like they're the same. No, the first question asks, "Whose are we going to be?" which means: Who is your audience? Who are you playing to? Who are you trying to gratify? I've said before that if you think your self-worth is a function of your performance plus the opinion of others, then you're caught in a trap that leaves your self-esteem up for grabs every single day. But if you're playing to a higher audience or higher set of values, that's a different thing. Now you can do what is right because you know it's the right thing to do, instead of being driven by other people's opinions of you. It's what allows you to act with integrity.

The second question has to do with who you are. What is your purpose? Why are you here? I think it's really important that we all think about why we are here and what we are trying to do. If you don't have a clear purpose, then you can be jerked around and taken in all kinds of directions because you don't really know why you're here.

If you can answer these questions and then can create some pictures in your mind of what it looks like when you are acting from that knowledge, you will be available to the joys and richness of living your life fully, moving full steam ahead.

Jim's message reminded me that the concepts we had discovered for creating a compelling vision were the same both for organizations and for individuals. Collectively and individually, we need a significant purpose, a picture of where we are going, and clear values. It gives meaning to our lives and provides direction. It helps us get focused, get energized, and get great results.

Blurry Vision

I had been working at the agency for over two months and was feeling pretty good. I liked working. I had a sense of accomplishment, liked the people I worked with, and felt good about bringing home a paycheck. My morning discussions with Jim were especially enriching.

Early Monday, I was sharing my reflections with Jim when my mobile phone rang. It was my son, Alex.

"Mom, don't be mad at me," he began. "I got in a fight with some boys on the way to school. I'm okay. I promise. I'm with a police officer right now. She wants to talk with you."

I caught my breath. *What was going on?*

"Your son appears to be all right," the officer said. "But he lost consciousness briefly and has a cut on his forehead. An ambulance is on the way. You can meet us at the hospital. I'd like to talk with you."

Feeling a rising panic, I hung up the phone.

"Alex is hurt. I'm going to the hospital," I said.

I stood up quickly, probably too quickly, because I got momentarily dizzy and had to sit back down.

"You don't look like you should be driving," Jim responded. "Where's your car? I'll drive you there."

I thanked him as we headed out the door.

While Jim drove, I told him what little I knew.

When we arrived at the hospital, Alex and the police officer were already there. Alex was in a room waiting for a doctor. When he turned and looked at me, I gasped. He was holding a bloody rag over his eye.

"Mom," he said, starting to cry. I put my arm around him and asked, "What happened?"

Alex was too upset to talk. He wasn't making any sense. At that point the doctor came in and began to examine him. The cut was right above Alex's eye.

"It's not a bad cut, but it will require stitches," the doctor said calmly. "And because you lost consciousness, Alex, we'll need to observe you overnight."

Stay overnight in the hospital? This was serious.

The police officer asked me if I could step outside to speak with her a moment. Alex was being attended to by the nurse and had stopped crying. Jim had been standing nearby the whole time, solid as a rock. He accompanied me out of the room.

The officer said, "Ma'am, from the report by the neighbor who called me—and from what I can tell at this point—your son was involved in a fight with three boys. One of them hit him in the face with a rock. When he fell to the ground, the boys ran off. The neighbor found him dazed. Alex says he doesn't remember much about the incident, but he told me that these boys have been harassing him for some time. I'd like to know what you've done about this situation so far."

I stood looking at her, speechless. *What had I done about the situation? How could I have done anything about the situation when I didn't even know about the situation?* I told her that this was the first I was hearing about anything.

She looked me over. I figured she was appraising me as a mother and I was coming up short. She said simply, "If you want to file a police report, you can call or come to the police station." She gave me her phone number and left.

Stunned, I turned and looked at Jim. He put his arm around my shoulder and said, "One thing at a time, Ellie. Let's see how Alex is doing."

We went back in the room. The rest of the day was a whirlwind. A surgeon stitched and dressed the wound. Alex was moved to a different room. He was put in a hospital gown, and I was handed his bloody clothes. Jim got a ride back to work so I would have my car. I spent most of the day at the hospital with Alex, but when I asked him about what had happened, he was uncommunicative. I figured he was drowsy from medication or just exhausted by all the events, so I didn't press for information. I spent the afternoon in his room watching him doze off and on.

• • •

I left around 6:00 to pick up Jen from debate club. When I told her what had happened to her brother, she was upset but, to my amazement, not surprised.

"I figured something like this was going to happen sooner than later. Maybe now someone will do something," she said angrily.

I didn't respond to her remark, assuming she was angry with the boys who'd hurt Alex and needed time to cool down. We ate dinner in silence, and then I went back to the hospital to sit with Alex. Alex slept while I thumbed through magazines. I left the hospital later, after the nurses assured me he would be fine through the night.

When I returned home, I poked my head into Jen's room and saw that she was asleep. I thought again about what she'd said earlier: *I figured something like this was going to happen sooner than later. Maybe now someone will do something.* She'd said the words with such anger in her voice. Had that anger been directed at me? I was sure my kids knew how much I loved them, but maybe I was out of touch with how they were feeling about me. Had I been misinterpreting their pulling away as a sign of independence, when in fact it was a sign that they were upset with me?

Getting ready for bed, I was struck by a blinding headache. I stumbled toward the medicine cabinet. As I glanced in the mirror, my vision blurred, and I could hardly see myself at all.

I spent much of the night awake, thinking about what was really going on at home and what I needed to do as a mother.

Sometimes it's painful to look at the truth. It's easier to hold on to our illusions of the way we want things to be. I had been telling myself that the

children were fine because they weren't complaining.
A good look in the mirror can be quite a shock.

• • •

I picked up Alex at the hospital early the next morning. I had arranged to take the day off from work. Alex
was subdued as we drove home. I didn't say much on
the ride, either. Once home, I made him breakfast.

I took a seat next to him at the table and said,
"Alex, I love you a lot. I'm not sure how much I've
been showing that to you lately. I want to know what's
going on because I care about you and want to help
you. Please tell me anything you want to—about our
family, about me as your mother, about school, about
the boys you got in the fight with. I want to listen and
I'm here."

Alex's jaw tightened, and his face grew red.

"You don't even care about what happens to me
anymore!" he yelled. "All you care about is work!
We're not a family anymore. I'm really, really alone,
and you just don't care."

"I'm sorry, Alex. I'm sorry." I took him in my arms,
and he began to sob.

When he was ready to talk, he said, "Some boys
started teasing me a couple of months ago. They made
fun of me because I was the only boy in the art club.
I stopped going to art club, but they didn't stop teasing me. I tried to ignore them. But the more I ignored
them, the nastier they got. Yesterday on my way to
school, they followed me and called me names again.
I'd had enough, so instead of ignoring them, I called

them names back. I used words you would never let me use, Mom. I thought that would stop them, but the next thing I knew, all three boys were on top of me beating me. I'm not even sure who hit me with the rock. I don't remember much after that. I think a woman ran out of a house, and the boys got scared and ran away. I think she called the police."

"Alex, why haven't you told me all of this was going on?"

He was silent for the longest moment, as if he were trying to avoid answering my question. I just waited, refusing to back down.

He finally said, "I've already told you, Mom. You're so busy with work all the time. Besides, I know you want me to handle my own problems."

"Does anyone know that this has been going on?" I asked.

"Jen knows, but nobody else."

"That must be why she wasn't surprised when I told her what had happened," I said. "In fact, she seemed more angry than upset."

"I think she *is* angry, Mom."

It was starting to sink in just how badly I had been shirking my responsibilities as a mother.

"We have two problems to solve, Alex. One problem is with these bullies. No one expects you to solve this kind of problem alone. I'm going to file the police report and get the boys' parents involved. I'll also let the school know what happened and will meet with them. I'm absolutely not going to allow any taunting or harassment to continue."

Alex looked relieved.

"The second problem is one that Jen, you, and I need to solve together. We need to talk about our family—about what has been happening to us and how we can make things better."

Later that afternoon, when Jen came home from school, Alex and I were waiting for her with fresh-baked cookies and milk. I'd had several hours to think about what was going on and decided that I needed to listen to the children. I announced that we needed to have a family meeting.

Jen really let me have it. In no uncertain terms, she told me what a rotten mother I had been. I could see that Alex was angry, too, although he hadn't expressed it as openly as Jen.

"Mom, it feels like you don't care about us anymore," Jen accused. "You don't cook meals anymore—you heat up frozen food or order pizza. You're always gone in the morning before I wake up. You don't notice when I'm getting ready for bed or kiss me good night!"

I told Jen I hadn't realized how bad things had been for her and Alex and how really sorry I was. I hugged her, wiped her tears, and said, "Sweetheart, things are going to change now."

Jen sniffled, "I miss the stories you used to make up."

I had to acknowledge that Jen was right. I had really been blowing things by ignoring the signals at home. My independent, self-reliant children really did need me, and I hadn't been there for them. I felt terrible.

After dinner, I broached the subject again with the children. "I've missed telling you stories. I'd like us to make up one together now—one about what kind of family we want to be. And then I'd like us to make it a true story."

I was amazed how resilient and forgiving my children were. They weren't nearly as hard on me as I was on myself. Once they knew I really cared about what they thought and wanted, their anger dissipated and a real conversation began.

"I'd like you to be around more," Alex said. "Even if I'm not talking with you, I like to know you're there."

"Yeah," said Jen. "You don't have to make my breakfast, but I'd like to at least see you in the morning when I get up. And I'd like to be able to kiss you good night."

"I'm happy to do that, sweetheart," I replied. "I was thinking you were both so grown up you didn't need me so much anymore."

"Mom," Jen said. "You've gone overboard on work and ignored us too much. But we don't want you to go overboard in the other direction, back to being Supermom. It's overwhelming when you're involved in every aspect of our lives."

I asked them what they wanted from me as their parent, and I shared what I thought a parent's role should be. We agreed that it wasn't good for parents to fix every problem because then children don't learn to solve their own problems. With the best of intentions I had done a little too much fixing over the years, and it hadn't been helpful. They wanted me to support them in learning how to solve their own problems, to offer encouragement and support, to allow them to fail and learn their own lessons, and to be judicious in offering advice. I said I thought I could do a better job of that. I said there were going to be times when I would have to step in whether they wanted me to or not. I told them I would still set limits and expectations and that they'd need to trust my judgment at those times.

"That's fine," Alex said. "We want you to be our mother, not our friend."

To my surprise, Alex and Jen stated their opinion that I "needed a life." They thought I should be dating more. I asked what would happen if I got involved in a serious relationship with a man. They said that they wanted me to be happy and that if I were involved with someone who made me happy, they would be happy also.

After the children went to bed, I realized we had discussed all three elements of a compelling vision. We had talked about what the purpose of our family was and why it was important. We had created a picture of what it would look like if we were really being the kind of family we wanted to be. We had talked about what our relationships would look like, what we would be doing, what we would be saying, what our home would look like, what kinds of activities we would do together, and what things we would do alone. We had shared what we each care deeply about, our most passionate values, how we hoped to act, how we wanted to be treated by each other, and what really pushed our buttons and violated our core values.

I wrote up a statement that summarized what we had discussed.

Later, as I prepared for bed, I realized the headache that had plagued me for most of the day was gone. I glanced in the mirror and saw a clear reflection smiling back at me.

At breakfast, I showed Jen and Alex what I had written. They thought it was a good summary of our discussion. They made a few minor changes, and Jen offered to type it up. She titled it "Our Family Vision" and put it on the refrigerator. It read:

Our Purpose (who we are)

Our purpose as a family is to support each other's growth, be there for each other, and contribute to our community.

Our Picture of the Future (where we're going)

Our picture of the future is that we will always be united through our love. Mom is a constant force in Alex and Jen's life, but not a micromanager. She is aware of how Alex and Jen are doing and expects us to do our best. She is a role model for us as a loving mother, working parent, and someone we can confide in. Jen and Alex contribute to the welfare of our family. They can be depended on to do their chores without being reminded. Our family contributes to worthy causes with donations and volunteer time. We dance, tell stories, and play games together. We learn from our mistakes and communicate upsets honestly and openly.

Our Values (what will guide our journey)

Our values are *love*, *respect*, *open communication*, and *fun*. We know we are acting on our values when we love each other as we are, when we treat each other as important members of the family, when we speak the truth in a way that others can hear, and when we play and laugh together. As we grow older, our love will always unite us.

We'd done it! We had created a family vision with a significant purpose, a picture of the future, and clear values. Because it was a shared vision, I knew we were all on the same boat together, able to move full steam ahead. What a relief!

I really didn't like having to give up my morning conversations with Jim, but I was absolutely certain that my family was—and had to be—the most important thing in my life. Period.

You Can't Get There Unless You're Here

After breakfast I dropped off the twins at school and headed to work. Later in the morning, I sent Jim an e-mail thanking him for his help and telling him briefly about the conversation with my children. I also said that I'd like to talk with him and asked him to call me at home after work.

That evening, Jim and I had a long talk on the phone. I told him in detail about my conversations with Jen and Alex, how I had taken a hard look in the mirror at myself as a mother, and about our new family vision. He was supportive and impressed. We agreed that an important part of having a vision was to be honest about the current realities. In fact, an honest and accurate assessment of the present is as important as a vision of the future. They go together.

"You can't get to the future without being present," Jim said.

"How true!" I said with a laugh. I heard a beep on the line.

"I'm getting another call that I need to take," said Jim, "but it will be brief. Can I put you on hold for a minute? I promise this won't take long."

"Sure," I said.

While I was on hold, I thought of Marsha, who had shown great leadership in creating a vision for the accounting department. She was proud of how we had redefined some of our processes to make them more user-friendly. The tension between the accountants and the agents seemed to have resolved; and surprisingly, Eugene and Darryl were actually good buddies. But there were still problems. One of the accountants in our department, Randy, was dropping the ball, and no one was confronting him. Everyone just worked around him, but it made things harder for the rest of us—and didn't seem right. It occurred to me that unless our department did an honest and accurate assessment of our current situation, we would never be able to fully achieve our vision. That's what happens when you focus on the future without also looking at the present.

Then I thought about the opposite kind of situation, where people focus on the present without a vision for the future. I thought of my friend's now-former husband. His energies had been focused on all the things that were wrong in his life. He was totally stuck in the present. His attitude had affected his work and marriage. He'd gone to counseling, but he was so totally stuck all he could see were problems, not any new possibilities. Eventually my friend couldn't take it any longer, and they divorced.

I realized that both of these views are important: a clear vision for the future and an honest, realistic view of the present.

"I'm back, Ellie," said Jim. "Are you still there?"

"Yes, I am." I replied. "More here than I've ever been."

"I've been thinking about how it's not enough to just have a vision. As your vision becomes clear, you have to look at your current reality and take stock. You have to maintain your focus on your vision and at the same time, without blaming yourself or anyone else, be honest about the truth of your present reality. Vision without being present is like having your head in the clouds. Holding the present without vision is like being stuck in the mud."

"You're right!" Jim responded. "I'm reminded of the *Titanic*. Now that was a powerful steamship! It was designed, developed, and launched with a clear vision of being the largest, most luxurious, strongest steamship ever. They were totally focused on their vision. But they didn't hold an honest account of their present realities. Aware of the icebergs, they made a terrible decision to hold to a time line while denying the danger of their current situation. And without enough life jackets and lifeboats, they were unprepared for the possibility of unforeseen circumstances. The disastrous result is an example of focusing on the vision without looking at the present at the same time."

"Doing both—focusing on your vision and being honest about the truth of your present situation—is what allows you to move full steam ahead," I concluded.

"Absolutely," Jim replied, adding:

> *Learn from the past,*
> *plan for the future, and*
> *live in the present.*

In other words: Live your vision now."

"Living my family's vision now means no more early-morning talks for us," I reflected. "Our morning conversations have meant so much to me. It's such a special time, and it really helps me start my day on a good note. I hate to give that time up. Realistically, though, I know that I need to be there for my children. That morning time is important to them, too."

I was hoping that Jim would come up with an alternative. As usual, he was open and honest.

"Ellie, our conversations have added a lot to both our lives and are important to both of us. I don't like the idea of giving up our morning time together, either, because it's such a perfect time for me, too. I do agree that your children come first. What if you had a family meeting with them and told them about our conversations and how important they have been to you? Would they be willing to let you come in early one morning a week? That might be a possible solution."

I agreed to talk with them. I knew that I would need to make sure they would be honest with me. Since honesty was part of our family vision, I could begin the conversation by reviewing the vision—that would set the stage for an open, honest problem-solving discussion. I could see that the family vision was going to be important for helping our family go forward.

"I've been thinking about Alex," Jim said. "You mentioned that he likes to draw but doesn't want to take art class right now because no other boys are in the class."

"That's right," I replied. "I really see him struggling with how much of his gentler side he wants to show. I think this thing with the bullies has made him feel he needs to show a tougher side."

"It would be a shame for him not to develop his talent," Jim continued. "My daughter, Kristen, will be home for the summer. She'll be working part-time at the agency in marketing. I think you know she's an art major. She might enjoy giving Alex some private art lessons. She's been a camp counselor in the past and has always enjoyed being with younger children, maybe because she doesn't have any siblings of her own. Do you think that might be a good idea?"

"It's a wonderful idea! Our family's vision says that we support one another's growth. This is a creative alternative that allows Alex to continue developing his art abilities and takes the pressure off while he's working out his issues with his image. Let's talk with Alex and Kristen and see what they think of the idea."

What an amazing thing about having a vision, I thought as Jim and I got off the phone. *If you are clear about your vision, and if you are honest about your present realities, you don't have to figure everything out. Things start happening of their own accord. What a gift!* I felt so grateful.

The children agreed that I could go in to work early one morning a week as long as it wasn't Monday. They wanted me home for the beginning of the week. Jim and I chose Tuesday as "our morning" and began a routine of weekly conversations.

Kristen did give art lessons to Alex that summer, and their relationship bloomed. She was an amazing young woman and a wonderful "big sister" to Alex, who really needed and benefited from her guidance and friendship.

20/20 Vision: Company, Team, and Personal Visions

Our Tuesday morning discussions became more focused. Jim was considering his vision for the agency. At the same time, I was working on my vision for my life.

I had gotten to know Jim and his family much better. Alex was at Jim's house frequently visiting Kristen. While dropping off Alex and picking him up, I often chatted with Jim's wife, Carolyn. One afternoon as I waited for Alex, Carolyn confided in me.

"I know you and Jim are talking about vision," she said. "This is so important for him. Until he creates his own vision for the agency, he'll always be living in his father's shadow."

Shortly after my conversation with Carolyn, I was chatting with Jim about vision.

"I think it's easier to have a vision when everything is going well," I said. "When I was younger, I thought I knew where I was going and was sure I was on the right path. I married, had children, and things were going according to plan. But when Doug died, I was overwhelmed by grief. I couldn't admit it, but I was also angry at him for dying and leaving me alone with so much responsibility. I dedicated the next thirteen years of my life to being a mother. It was the only identity I had. Thinking back, I realize I didn't really have a vision. It was just a plan I hadn't given much thought to. If I'd had a vision, it could have guided me through those hard times, helped me create a life for myself, and helped me be a better mother. I would have noticed sooner that my long hours at work were taking me in the wrong direction from my family."

After a prolonged silence, Jim acknowledged, "The same is true for me. I always knew that someday I would take over the business from my father. Everyone in my family wanted it, and I think I wanted it, too. Or at least I never considered anything else. So maybe that was a vision. But it wasn't a clear vision— because here I am now, president of the company, and I can't seem to make it shine the way my father did. A vision should guide you. I feel like I'm going one step at a time, but I'm not sure where it's leading."

I smiled at Jim. Touched by his frankness and honesty and remembering what Carolyn had told me, I said, "Jim, I think you *do* know what your vision for the company is."

• • •

It occurred to me that Jim already had identified the elements of his vision, but he didn't realize it, because

he hadn't put it all together. I decided to remind him
and see if putting it together might inspire him.

"The first week I met you, you told me the purpose
of your agency. Remember? You said you were in the
'financial peace-of-mind' business—that the agency
provided customers with financial security for possible
worst-case scenarios. It also provided customers with
the security of knowing they will be supported if they
need to place a claim. Right?"

"That's right," Jim replied. "It's something I
learned from my father."

"Do you believe it yourself?" I asked.

"Absolutely. Knowing we have a worthwhile purpose motivates me to work in the family business."

"When we discussed picture of the future, you saw
happy customers."

"That's right. They had the best insurance for
their situation at the best price, and when there was a
problem, they only needed to make one call—to us."

"Also, you identified the values you believe are needed
to guide people as they pursue that purpose, right?"

"Right again," Jim replied. "The values are *integrity, relationships,* and *success.*"

"So you do have the essence of a compelling vision," I said. "It seems to me all you need to do is put it
together. So, tell me, what does it look like when everyone in the agency is guided by the vision and living
it consistently?"

Jim chuckled and said, "Okay, Ellie. I'll tell you.

"My vision is that our customers feel peace of
mind knowing they have financial security for possible

worst-case scenarios and that they will be supported if they need to place a claim. Our customers trust that everyone in our company has their best interest in mind. They have friendly relationships with the agents who take the time to understand what they need. Our agents find them exactly what they need at the best price. When our customers need to make a claim, they only need to make one call—to us. We take it from there. That same sense of trust permeates the agency. Every department and every individual is clear about how they contribute to our vision. We trust each other to follow through on commitments and treat each other with mutual respect. We're clear about our roles, and we hold ourselves and each other accountable. We're committed to getting our egos out of the way and working through disagreements with our customers in mind. We're knowledgeable and competent in negotiating the most benefits for the lowest price for our customers, and we provide unparalleled service for them as we settle their claims.

"If we do this, our customers will be our number one marketers; 100 percent will recommend us to their friends and relatives. Our agency will be recognized by the city as an important contributor to our community. Every single person who works here will come to work each day enthusiastic about being here."

"That's inspiring, Jim," I said. "I don't think I've ever heard you speak so passionately before about the company. You included everything—purpose, picture of the future, and values. And it works! How do you feel?"

"I feel inspired," Jim responded. "It's interesting. I sound like my father in terms of his energy and enthusiasm. But these are my words, not his. I've described a vision that will guide our people. They won't be dependent on me to keep them focused and motivated. The sparkle and energy will come from them, living the shared vision."

"I bet your dad would be really proud of you."

"You know, I bet he would be," Jim replied.

• • •

While Jim continued to contemplate his vision for the company and how to move forward with it, those of us in the accounting department were moving forward on our vision under Marsha's leadership. Marsha said she had heard too many people complain over the years that they couldn't have a vision because their company didn't have one. She didn't believe that. She moved forward because we had an urgent need for a vision and no time to wait for the rest of the company. From what I could tell, our accounting department vision was having a positive effect on the rest of the company by improving our relationship with other departments and serving as a model for how to create a vision.

Marsha told us she wasn't concerned about getting ahead of the rest of the company, because if and when a company-wide vision emerged, our team could easily revisit our department vision to align it with the company vision.

Our team demonstrated:

*You don't have to wait
for the company to have a vision.
Vision can start anywhere.*

• • •

Over the next few weeks as Jim contemplated his vision, I focused on my personal vision. Now that I had seen the power of a shared vision for my family, I was more motivated than ever to create a vision for myself. I had started this job with the attitude that I was at the threshold of creating my own life. Although I enjoyed working at the agency, what I liked best were the people and not the work itself. I still wasn't sure where my life was heading.

I had figured out this much: My vision needed to be about the *quality* of the life I wanted to live and not about the specifics. I had a friend who was sure she would never be fulfilled unless she could find the right husband. Another friend was certain she would never be fulfilled unless she had children. Another friend believed that he would never be fulfilled unless he got a PhD. I noticed that people got attached to specific goals as though they not only *represented* the vision but *were* the vision. And often, once they achieved the goal, they weren't satisfied.

• • •

One Tuesday morning I said to Jim, "I think I've figured out what my personal purpose and picture of the future are."

"What are they?" asked Jim.

"My purpose is to 'Help myself and others learn and express fundamental truths about ourselves and the world.'"

"That sounds pretty good," said Jim. "What's your picture of the future? What does it look like when you are fulfilling your purpose?"

"I think I'm fulfilling my purpose when something is expressed. It's not just when something is learned; it's when something new is created."

"That's a good start," said Jim. "How about your values?"

"That's where I need some help," I said. "The values of the agency make sense to me and guide me at work, but are these the same as my personal values?"

"No," Jim replied. "The values of the agency work for you because they are aligned with your personal values. That's why you fit in here so well. But your personal values reflect what *you* care most deeply about."

"I remember how impressed I was when you shared your values in a voice mail message. How did you identify them?" I asked.

"That's not difficult. We all have values, whether we've spent time putting them into words or not. To find out what you value, ask yourself questions such as, 'What do I care deeply about?' or 'What do I stand for?'"

"When we discussed our values for the accounting department, I wanted to include 'having fun,'" I said. "So I guess that's one of my values."

"It might be. We all value many things, but what do you value most? What are you willing to put yourself on the line for? By being conscious about these core values, we can be intentional about the choices we make in our lives.

"A technique that might help you identify your values is called the Three Whys. Identify what you think is a value and ask yourself, "Why do I value that?' Or 'If I had that, then what would I have?' Whatever the answer is, ask the question again. Do it three times. It will take you deeper to what's most important to you. And as you go deeper, you will feel a stronger sense of caring. The more deeply you care, it means you're closer to your core values."

I spent the rest of the week experimenting with the Three Whys. *What do I really value and why? When I get down to the core, what really matters most to me and why? What is absolutely essential to who I am? What do I stand for?*

I thought of a friend who had told me he valued money. I wondered how he would answer the Three Whys. Was money really a value for him, or did it represent something deeper? Power, perhaps? Status? Achievement? Control over his destiny?

I became aware of three values that I held most dearly: *truth, loving relationships*, and *creative expression*. The following week I shared my values with Jim:

> *Truth:* I know I am living by this value when I turn toward truth, even when I am afraid.

> *Loving relationships:* I know I am living by that value when I seek and sustain loving relationships with family and friends.

Creative expression: I know I am living by this value when the expression of what I create touches others in a deep and meaningful way, helping them to discover what they are ready to learn and to appreciate our commonalities as human beings.

"Those values make sense to me," Jim commented. "I suspect it was your value of *truth* that drove you to listen to your children when they were upset."

He continued, "Now I'm going to ask you to do the same thing you asked me to do—put it all together. What's your vision? Try writing for a few minutes and see what you come up with."

I laughed and took the challenge. After a few minutes I looked up and said, "How does this sound?"

Through observing and being present, I help myself and others bring their hopes and dreams to a conscious level in order to understand and express them. The expression of what I create touches others in a deep and meaningful way, helping them to discover what they are ready to learn and to appreciate our commonalities as human beings. I turn toward truth, even when I am afraid. With an open heart, I help create an environment where people can be their best selves. I seek and sustain loving relationships with family and friends. With compassion, I take responsibility for my mistakes and learn from them. I model that the best way to control my destiny is to let go of control and to appreciate and actualize the gifts I have been given.

"Beautiful," Jim replied. "Your vision itself is a creative expression."

He paused a moment and continued, "It does make me wonder, though, how your vision fits with working in an accounting department. It's not the kind of place you can express your creative side."

An astute observation, I thought. It was true that my greatest joy came from writing the stories my kids had enjoyed so much over the years.

"I noticed you stated your vision in present tense," Jim observed. "You didn't say 'I will.' How come?"

"When I think about the future, it's always 'out there'—it never arrives. I wanted to support my picture of the future by thinking about it as a reality right now. I imagine there are a lot of ways, though, to express personal vision."

"That reminds me of a story I read about Alfred Nobel, father of the Nobel Peace Prize," Jim commented. "When his brother died, Nobel picked up a Swedish newspaper to see what they had written about him. The paper had gotten the two brothers confused, so Alfred Nobel read his own obituary instead. Alfred Nobel was one of the inventors of dynamite, so his obituary was all about dynamite and destruction. He was just devastated. Later, when his friends and loved ones gathered, Alfred asked them, 'What do you think is the opposite of destruction?' They all agreed it was peace. Right then he decided to chart a new course for his life so he would be remembered for peace."

"So an obituary could be an expression of a picture of the future," I remarked.

"It could," Jim replied thoughtfully.

• • •

The next morning, Jim handed me a typed page.

"Read this," he said with a smile.

He had written his own obituary! I read it with interest.

> Jim Carpenter was a loving teacher and example of simple truths, whose leadership helped himself and others awaken the presence of God in their lives. He was a caring child of God, a son, brother, spouse, father, grandfather, father-in-law, brother-in-law, godfather, uncle, cousin, friend, and business colleague, who strove to find a balance between success and significance. He was able to say no in a loving manner to people and projects that got him off purpose. He was a person of high energy who was able to see the positive in any event or situation. No matter what happened, he could find a "learning" or a message in it. Jim valued integrity; his actions were consistent with his words, and he was a mean, lean, 185-pound, flexible golfing machine. He will be missed because wherever he went, he made the world a better place by his having been there.

"Guess you're going to have to start working on your golf game," I teased. "Sounds like you're doing pretty well with the rest."

"I put the golf game in because I want to maintain my health and continue to enjoy sports."

"Your pictures of the future create meaning for you, just as mine do," I said.

"You're right," Jim replied. "My personal vision might not inspire or have meaning for anyone else, but it means a lot to me."

...

"I've been thinking about your personal vision some more," Jim said during our next Tuesday morning conversation. "It's clear that your talents and interest lie more in creative expression than in the world of numbers. Why do you work in the accounting department?"

I explained that I actually didn't like working with numbers that much, even though I was good with them. I had gotten a college degree in business because I thought it would give me security. I had gotten the job in the accounting department for the same reason. It was something I knew how to do.

"What I would really love to do is write," I told Jim. "But I don't have training and don't know what kind of job I could get doing it. And to be honest, I don't want to leave the agency."

"I think you should talk with Marsha about your concerns. I hear there's an opening in the marketing department. I think it would be a good fit with your talents, especially since you understand the purpose of our business so well."

Within a few weeks, I was working in the marketing department. It meant starting at the bottom doing mostly copyediting and formatting, but I was learning things that would help me further develop my real talents and passion.

Making life even more interesting, around the same time I started dating Sam, a man I'd met through a mutual friend. I had no idea what would become of the relationship, but I was having fun.

Creative Tension

I had already discovered the importance of focusing my vision and, at the same time, being honest about the present. I now realized that when I was willing to live with the tension this generated, opportunities seemed to appear almost as if by magic. Of course, admitting the truth about the present sometimes made me uncomfortable. It had been painful to acknowledge that I had fallen short in my role as a mother. But by being clear about what was important and being honest about the present, I was able to make a shift. Our family was thriving in wonderful new ways.

The same was true for my work. I hadn't wanted to be honest with myself that I wasn't happy in the accounting department because I was afraid it would mean I'd have to look for another employer—not to mention lose my enriching conversations with Jim. But as I maintained my focus on what was important and also what was real, an unexpected opportunity in the marketing department surfaced.

My newly developing relationship with Sam was also a mystery to me. Why had someone so interesting suddenly appeared in my life when no one had appealed to me for fifteen years?

"I believe these shifts came about because of my willingness to experience and live with the tension generated from focusing on both my vision and the truth about the present," I said to Jim during one of our conversations.

"I know what you mean," Jim replied. "After all that talking we did about the agency's vision, I found that I wanted to just sit with it a while before I took action. I needed time to consider it, test my commitment to it, and think about it more deeply."

"At times, for me, the tension of holding an honest view of both my present and my vision is frightening. It feels like jumping off a cliff with no assurance of a safe landing," I said.

"Fortunately," I continued, "one of the lessons I learned from my father helps me remember how important it is not to resist the tension. As a child, I joined Dad on his fishing expeditions. I noticed that when hooked on a line, the fish usually pulled against the tension of the line. Dad played a game with the fish, letting the line out and pulling it in until the fish was worn out and then easily reeled in. But sometimes a smart fish didn't play the game. The smart fish swam toward the pole, keeping the tension loose until it found a way to get off the hook."

"Interesting. How do you apply that lesson?" Jim asked.

"I'm learning to be like the smart fish—to swim toward the hook instead of away from it. When I resist the truth about my current reality, I pull against the tension, which wears me out and prevents me from creating my desired future. By being honest about my present—accepting the tension and uncomfortable feelings—I can focus on my vision and discover new options."

"So it's all about feeling the tension and staying open to possibilities, is that it?" asked Jim.

"Only if you want to be a smart fish," I quipped.

From Vision to Reality: The Three Hows

Jim and I achieved what we had initially agreed to do: We identified the three key elements of a compelling vision. We were both pleased with what we had accomplished.

One Tuesday morning, we sat quietly looking at each other over our cups of coffee.

"It's one thing to identify the vision," Jim remarked. "It's another to make it happen. I'm clear about my vision for the agency, but most people in the company are not on board yet. I've been talking about it a lot, but I don't think people are really getting it the way I want them to. I want them to be excited about it. I want them to feel a sense of ownership for making it come alive."

"So you're saying that coming up with a great vision that includes all three elements is not enough," I said.

"Right," said Jim. "I've thought about having marketing create something so everyone could have a copy."

"I'd enjoy working on that project," I replied. "But I'm not sure it would give people the sense of ownership you're looking for."

"You're right," said Jim. "If people don't buy into it, it's likely to be framed and forgotten."

We came up with a motto:

Vision is a lot more than putting
a plaque on the wall.
A real vision is lived, not framed.

"So how do you turn a vision into reality?" I wondered. "Apparently writing one down and telling people about it are not enough."

I thought about the vision I had created with my children for our family. It struck me that the discussions we had in shaping the vision were as powerful as the vision itself. If I had presented to my children the exact same vision without involving them in creating it, I doubted that it would have meant as much to them. The same was true with the vision we had created for the accounting department. We had worked together as a team to craft our vision. It occurred to me that Jim hadn't engaged others in real dialogue and given them an opportunity to help shape the vision.

"I don't think you can just go out and announce your new vision and expect everyone to immediately understand it or agree with it," I commented. "You need to look at who should be involved in shaping the vision, and you have to be open to their thoughts, dreams, hopes, and needs. You have to be willing to allow others to help shape it."

"You're right," Jim agreed. "So 'how it's created' is as important as what it says."

"Exactly," I replied.

"I also think how it's communicated is important," Jim said. "Even if people aren't involved in shaping the vision, they need to understand how it relates to their situation."

"And what it means to live it," I added.

Jim took out a note card and wrote the following:

THE THREE HOWS
FOR MAKING YOUR VISION A REALITY

- How it's created

- How it's communicated

- How it's lived

When he finished writing, Jim tacked the note card on the wall above the elements of a compelling vision.

"For the past six months, we've worked on identifying the elements of a compelling vision, and we've done a great job," Jim said. "But it's not enough. For our vision to become a reality, we need to understand these 'Three Hows.'"

"So we can move full steam ahead, all on the same boat," I said with a smile.

How It's Created

The next time we met, Jim began the conversation by saying, "I understand that others need to be involved in shaping the vision. I'm okay with sharing my vision with others and listening to their thoughts and reactions. But how much do I allow others to have input? I'm pretty passionate about it. To be honest, I don't know how much I'm willing to change it."

I thought about the vision of Dr. Martin Luther King, Jr. It really wasn't just his vision alone. His vision expressed the hopes and dreams of millions of people.

"I think it's your job as the leader of this company to ensure there's a shared vision, to champion the vision, but not to *own* the vision," I offered. "Everyone in the company must own the vision. Otherwise, it's just your vision and not a shared vision. The more involved people are in creating it, the more they will feel a sense of ownership—then it's not just your vision; it's everyone's vision."

"That makes sense," Jim replied. "But also I think leaders are supposed to know where they're going. If

I don't tell them what the vision is, they'll lose confidence in me. On the other hand, if they don't agree with my vision, it doesn't matter how passionate I am—it's not going to happen."

"Sounds like a dilemma," I reflected. "I wonder if it has to be either/or. Take a look at the accounting department. Don't you find it interesting that a department in a company has been able to create an exciting vision when the larger company doesn't have one?"

"Good point," Jim remarked. "It's obvious that the people in Marsha's department are energized and enthusiastic. They work well with each other as well as with other departments."

• • •

Later that day as I walked through the lunchroom, I noticed Jim and Marsha in deep conversation. As I passed their table, Marsha looked up.

"Hey, Ellie," she said, "Why don't you join us? We're having an interesting conversation about one of your favorite topics—vision."

"I was just asking Marsha how the accounting department created their vision," Jim said.

I took a seat at their table as Marsha responded to Jim's question.

"First I encouraged my team to honestly share with each other their hopes and dreams for the future. Through these discussions, we discovered the common threads and developed the shared vision together."

"Weren't you concerned that we might come up with something you couldn't support?" I asked.

"Not really," Marsha replied. "If something was fundamentally at odds with what I felt was important, then I always had veto power."

"How did the process work for you?" Jim asked.

Marsha smiled as she answered, "Actually, I found the team-developed vision was better than what I would have come up with on my own. I discovered that when you allow others to be involved in shaping the vision, they bring a wider range of perspectives that enrich the vision."

"I was impressed with everyone's contributions. The different perspectives added depth. I think we all learned a lot from each other and developed more respect and appreciation for each other in the process," I added.

"That makes sense," Jim said. "The people here are intelligent, have a lot of experience, and really care about the future of the agency. I don't think it's a risk to involve them. What do you think, Marsha?"

"I think it might be a risk not to," she replied.

The next time we met, Jim and I reflected on the importance of involving others in shaping the vision. We realized:

> *The process of creating the vision*
> *is as important as what the vision says.*

• • •

Over the next several months, instead of simply publishing the vision, Jim brought in an experienced facilitator who led a series of company-wide meetings. These were not the typical business meetings where the leaders made presentations while everyone else listened. These meetings were designed so that people participated in real dialogue about the vision and had many opportunities to give feedback. Jim encouraged everyone to voice their ideas and concerns.

Initially a few people were skeptical, saying things like, "We've already done this stuff, and it's a waste of time." Or, "Wait him out—then things will get back to normal." Maybe they were concerned that they might have to change or they would lose something. What they didn't realize was how absolutely and totally committed Jim was to this process. Eventually they got the message.

The majority of us sincerely engaged in the dialogues right from the start. Those in the accounting department were especially enthusiastic, as they understood from experience how powerful this process was and were excited about the opportunity to connect their vision for their department to the agency's vision.

After lively discussions around purpose and picture of the future, Jim articulated three values that he believed were fundamental to guiding our purpose as an agency: *integrity, relationships,* and *success.* During our discussions, we debated whether to add to or change any of these. We also discussed what order they should be listed in. Many people felt that financial success should be ranked above relationships, but Jim was adamant on this and eventually convinced us that if we didn't take care of each other and our customers through building strong relationships, we wouldn't be truly successful. He explained that our purpose in providing peace of mind might mean taking a short-term financial loss at times, but our vision was about the long term. It was impressive hearing these thoughts coming from the president of the company. We did decide to change the word *integrity* to *ethical behavior*. We also further defined the values, so we could have a shared understanding of exactly what they meant. In this way we would be better able to hold ourselves and each other accountable. After many discussions and lots of shared feedback, we agreed on the following:

1. Ethical Behavior
   - Be truthful and fair when dealing with others, legal in our practices, and able to be proud if our actions were publicized.
   - Practice what we preach: Our behavior models our products and services.
   - Be trustworthy. Say what we mean; do what we say.
2. Relationships
   - Make and keep our commitment to colleagues, customers, the company, our community, and ourselves, and cheer each other on in the process.

- Show respect for ourselves and others by listening and being supportive, and by addressing and resolving conflicts.
- Appreciate and utilize diversity so we make smarter decisions and so each person has the opportunity to maximize his or her potential.

3. Success

- Contribute to the growth and prosperity of our company, community, and the environment.
- Pursue excellence in doing worthwhile, high-quality work.

People in the company saw that Jim and the senior leaders were committed to a collaborative process in creating our vision. By involving us in clarifying our purpose, picture of the future, and values—rather than presenting those to us—more and more people became honestly engaged. A momentum built. The more we shared our hopes and dreams and the more we were included in making decisions, the more excited we became.

•••

Seeing the difference between what we wanted and how we were currently operating as a company, some people wanted to start making changes right away in order to fix the problems. Jim explained that many of the suggestions for major changes, such as reorganization, needed to be thought through more carefully. He encouraged people to live with the creative tension as they continued to take an honest look at their present realities and discuss their hopes and dreams for the future.

On the other hand, Jim and others did take action on "low-hanging fruit"—obvious things that could easily and quickly be improved. Meanwhile, the more serious issues with larger implications were studied during that period until they were more fully understood.

Some changes happened naturally. A few people decided that the vision didn't fit with their personal goals or with their beliefs of where the agency should be going. They left the agency. Others who had been resistant at first became enthusiastic leaders once they realized that the ship was really moving full steam ahead.

Through our sincere conversations about the future of the agency, all of us were creating a shared view of our desired future. Because everyone was involved in some way in the discussions shaping the vision, once it was finalized, it was easy to communicate it. Everyone already understood it and had a deep sense of ownership for it.

During that time, every department in the agency started working on their vision for their team. They created visions that were specific to their team but that were also aligned with the vision for the agency. Marsha acted as a resource to the team leaders, sharing what we had done in the accounting department.

"Things are really starting to shift," Jim said during one of our Tuesday conversations. "I'm beginning to see the energy and sparkle I've been looking for."

I couldn't remember ever seeing him look happier.

How It's Communicated

One morning Jim and I were chatting about the length of the vision statement, which was almost two pages long.

"It's hard to remember all two pages," Jim commented.

"Once you really understand it, you don't have to come up with all the words," I said. "You can create a rallying call. Do you recall the old commercials for Ford Motor Company when they were beginning to seriously compete with Japan?" I asked.

"I sure do," he responded. "'Quality Is Job One.'"

"I grew up in Michigan," I continued, "so I'm very aware of the automotive industry. I was impressed with their rallying call. To most people 'Quality Is Job One' sounds like they're saying, 'Quality is the most important job.' And they are. But it's also a message that conveys deeper meaning. Most people don't know this, but Job One is the term for the first car off the assembly line. This car has to be perfect because it is used as the standard against which all of the other cars are built. When workers at Ford Motor first heard

'Quality Is Job One,' what they really heard was that every car they produced had to be perfect, held to the standard of the first job—the first car off the assembly line. They had a clear picture of what quality looks like. The rallying call also told them that they are going to seriously compete with the Japanese market in the area of quality. There was a lot of meaning attached to their rallying call, and it connected them to a shared vision. That was the year that the Ford Taurus overtook the Honda Accord as the best-selling car in that class."

"I remember when that happened," Jim responded. "The Japanese cars had dominated the market until that time. It was a huge turning point. Ford's vision allowed it to go full steam ahead!"

"But what happened?" I wondered. "It lasted for a while, but it didn't seem to fit anymore."

"There was a point in time when that vision didn't guide them anymore," Jim replied. "And that was a problem. When people lose sight of the vision or stop acting in concert with it, the rallying call becomes meaningless and actually turns people off."

"Maybe that's the difference between a rallying call that guides people and a slogan that is more for marketing purposes," I mused.

"I agree," Jim replied. "A rallying call needs to speak to the people in the organization to help them remember the vision—not just be solely a marketing message. I think a company could get into trouble if its rallying call wasn't shared throughout the company. Instead of exciting people, the rallying call would probably turn them off by showing how leadership is disconnected from the rest of the company."

"Here's a good one: Ritz-Carlton's 'We are ladies and gentlemen serving ladies and gentlemen,'" I offered.

"Another good one is Steve Jobs's vision to make computers accessible and affordable for everyone by creating a world with 'a computer on every desk,'" Jim added.

"How important is it to create a rallying call?" I wondered.

"Well, I think it's a 'nice to have' but not a 'necessary to have,'" replied Jim. "I'm glad our company is excited about our rallying call—being in the financial peace-of-mind business. I think the most important thing is to keep the vision alive. But whether we have a rallying call or not, it's essential to find ways to keep communicating about the vision."

"The more you focus on the vision, the clearer it becomes and the more deeply you understand it," I observed. "When we wrote our family vision, I knew some aspects might change over time, but the essence of the vision would remain."

"Good point, Ellie," Jim replied. "Vision shouldn't be a one-time activity."

We had uncovered another important principle:

Visioning is an ongoing process;
you need to keep talking about it.

Believing that communicating the vision was one of his most important jobs as a leader, Jim employed every means possible to do so. He spoke about it in his daily conversations with people. He included it as a topic during meetings, and he continued to refer to it in his daily voice mail. He encouraged other leaders to refer to the vision as part of their regular work so it would become integrated into the business and the way of doing business.

A cross-functional, cross-level communications team was set up to determine strategies to promote company-wide communications around the vision. They created a weekly newsletter with information and feedback that tracked our progress. They also created a social networking site where we could interact around the vision.

• • •

"All this stuff we've been doing has made me reconsider the role of leadership," Jim commented one morning. "As I've said before, I think leadership is about going somewhere. When I first took over as president, I wanted to be a good manager. I think I became one. Then I wanted to create a shared vision. Now that we have a shared vision, I'm not so sure about my role anymore."

I said, "So you're wondering since everyone owns the vision, how do the leaders help us?"

"Right. My father was the 'glue'—he had a charismatic personality that held us all together. Now we have a vision, and that is the glue. I don't need to inspire everyone the way my father did—the vision does that."

I offered, "Well, it's a good idea to remind us of what's important about the vision and help keep us on course by removing obstacles."

Jim laughed. "Of course. Focusing on the vision is what's important. It's so easy for leaders to fall into the trap of thinking that their people should be focused on them. When you have a shared vision, you can't maintain that viewpoint. The leader becomes a servant of the vision, not an important leader who needs to be served.

"I met the chairman of the board of Matsushita Electric when I was in Japan a number of years ago. He was eighty-eight years old at the time. One of the people I was with asked him, 'Sir, what is your primary job as chairman of the board of this great international company?'

"He didn't hesitate. He said, 'To model love. I am the soul of this company. It is through me that our organization's values pass.'

"I really liked that," Jim concluded. "When you shift from a self-oriented perspective, it changes the way you think about leadership. From this viewpoint, leadership is about serving the greater good. There is no room for ego-driven leadership."

I smiled and summarized. "So you're saying there are some important roles for leaders. One of your jobs is to remind people about what's really important. Another is to help them stay focused on the vision. Another is to remove obstacles whenever possible. And another is to encourage them to act and cheer them on."

Later that morning, I wasn't surprised at all to hear Jim's morning message.

Good morning, everyone. This is Jim. I've been thinking about my role as a leader in support of our vision. It's important for me to be a champion for our vision and to help keep it in front of us. It's my job to help you do your job. In that way, it is my job to serve you, so you can serve your customer. It's not your job to serve upper management. If I ever get confused and give the wrong message, please let me know.

• • •

Communication around the vision was central to the company's growth strategy. One of the most important aspects of communication was to help people interpret events in light of the vision. During a downturn in the economy, people were worried. Did this mean we were going under? During this period, Jim shared information with us on a regular basis that demonstrated that although we were cutting back in some areas, our vision was still the driving force for our agency. Communication around current events in relation to our vision allowed us to understand how we were continuing to move forward during adverse times and helped us stay committed. We came out of the downturn ready to continue full steam ahead.

A growth strategy was adopted to build stronger relationships with commercial customers, while maintaining the personal relationships with individual customers. The company began a phase of growth through acquisitions. Because of the open communications, everyone in the company understood how this strategy supported our vision, so they in turn supported it.

When searching for companies to acquire, leaders used our articulated values to evaluate potential candidates in order to ensure a good fit.

The mergers with the new companies went smoothly because we were able to easily and consistently communicate our vision—our purpose, picture of the future, and values.

How It's Lived

$\longrightarrow$

One Tuesday morning Jim and I talked again about how articulating a compelling vision and coming up with a catchy rallying call were not enough.

"This is where the rubber meets the road," Jim said. "How is your vision lived on a daily basis? There is no doubt in my mind that once you identify your vision, you have to start living it immediately and behaving consistently with the intention of that vision."

"That's so true," I said. "As soon as I realized I had been ignoring my children's needs, I had to stop. I couldn't say, 'I'll start being a better mother next week.' It's not easy, because sometimes it means making tough decisions. But I learned that the best thing for me, my children, my friends, and my coworkers was to live my values and to make choices based on them."

"I wish I could do that with my weight issues," Jim said. "Even though one of my values is health, I tend to have an 'I'll start next week' attitude on that one. Then again, everyone gains a little weight when they get older."

"What is your exercise program?" I asked.

"Exercise program?" Jim replied.

"Yes," I chided. "We cannot achieve our vision unless we help ourselves and each other act on our good intentions by setting up processes and systems that are aligned with the vision and help us stay on track. I consider these 'supporting structures.'

"What *supporting structure* do you have in place that supports your value of health? I know you eat healthy food, so that structure is in place. And I know you play golf any chance you can get. But I'm not sure what you do regularly for exercise."

He sheepishly admitted that he had tried several different approaches to exercise but lost interest in them because they weren't fun, or he was too busy, or it wasn't convenient. I pointed out that these all sounded like excuses. He admitted that they were.

"Is health really a value?" I asked. "Or is it just an interest?"

He replied, "Yes, it's a value, and I'm feeling bad that I'm not acting consistently with it."

Then I had a great idea. "I'm not doing well in the exercise department, either. Maybe we could set up a structure that would help both of us. Instead of talking over coffee on Tuesday mornings, how about if we walked together?"

As a result of that conversation, we set up a structure that supported our value of health, and we held each other accountable. Our Tuesday morning routine shifted once again as we continued our conversations during a brisk forty-five-minute walk.

• • •

During one of our walks Jim commented, "Our walks have made a big difference to me. I can see how supporting structures have helped me be accountable to my vision at the personal level. I assume they're important at the team level and organizational level, too."

"That's certainly true for teams," I replied. "I learned the importance of supporting structures from Marsha. Once the accounting department had a shared vision, everyone was quite excited. Some things improved naturally on their own, like the relationship between the accountants and the agents. But I remember—back when you and I were discussing creative tension—how Marsha was ignoring some problems that weren't resolving on their own, and it was beginning to affect morale. We had no way to hold someone accountable when they weren't behaving consistently with the vision. It certainly was beginning to create tension on the team."

"What happened?" Jim asked with curiosity.

"There was an uncomfortable team meeting where people started talking about their frustrations. Marsha realized that ignoring the behavior of those who act inconsistently with the vision threatens the trust and commitment of the rest of the team. She set up a supporting structure. She met with each of her direct reports to set written performance objectives with clear measures that included acting on the values as well as delivering results. She then met with each regularly to track performance and to provide whatever direction and support was needed. I remember thinking that one person, who was kind of a slacker in the department, would either quit or be fired, now that he was under the microscope. Instead, I was surprised to see him get refocused and become a productive member of the team."

"I know she put some other structures in place also. Now I see how important it was for her to do that," Jim remarked.

"Yes," I replied. "She wanted us to be a high-performing team, where we shared leadership and responsibility for prioritizing projects, coordinating our efforts, and solving problems. The communication and decision-making processes we set up were supporting structures that helped us stay on track as a team."

"Realizing that supporting structures are also important at an organizational level helps me understand what company-wide changes need to be made. I had waited a while after creating the vision to decide how to best move forward," Jim noted.

"Some of our policies and procedures are antiquated and are making getting the job done harder instead of easier. We're reexamining the agency's policies and procedures to ensure they are aligned with our vision. Those were easy decisions to make.

"Now there are some bigger issues to tackle. For example, we found that our information practices are great. People really do have access to the information they need. On the other hand, people are being

rewarded for individual contributions that don't encourage a team approach. We're creating a new reward
and compensation plan that supports both individual
and team contributions. I need to communicate to
HR that it's a priority. We've also decided to provide
training in team skills instead of just blaming people
for not being team players. Now that I see this is a
supporting structure and not just soft-skills training,
I need to reexamine the budget and make sure there is
adequate funding."

"Supporting structures help us set clear goals," I
observed.

"That's why I'm so excited about it," said Jim.
"Now that we have an organizational vision, our goals
have real meaning. Out of context, goals can seem
random or too abstract to care much about. But when
people see our goals as the building blocks for delivering on our vision, they become the milestones that let
us know we're on track. They're the specific, measurable actions we take as we move forward toward making our vision a reality."

• • •

We had learned some important steps on how to live a
vision. I wrote them on a note card and gave it to Jim
later that day:

STEPS TO MAKING YOUR VISION A REALITY

- Create a vision that illuminates purpose, a picture of the future, and values.

- Honestly assess your current situation, and be willing to live with the creative tension.

- Create supporting structures that are aligned with the vision.

- Set goals and action plans.

• • •

One morning Jim and I were discussing the importance of living our vision moment by moment. As we walked briskly up a hill on a new route, Jim reflected, "You know, Ellie, our walks make a nice metaphor for what we've learned about making vision a reality."

I glanced over at Jim, thinking he was probably onto something. But I was a little too out of breath to respond.

"Here's what I mean," he continued. "We know where we're going. And we've planned the route. But the only thing that is really important is the step you're taking right now. I mean that—literally. The step you are taking right now is the only thing there is. So how you take that step is really important. Are you present? Do you smell this fresh air? Do you hear the birds chirping? Do you feel the pavement under your feet? Are you living your vision right this moment?"

That stopped me short, because I actually had been thinking about making dinner, carpooling, and solving a work-related problem. I hadn't been experiencing the present moment at all. I realized that he was absolutely right. I was struck by how much of my time I spent thinking about the future rather than consciously living my vision in the present.

The rest of our walk was truly amazing as we took in the beauty of the early morning.

A couple of hours later, I listened to Jim's message and was deeply touched.

Good morning, everyone. This is Jim. I've been thinking about our vision and how important it is for all of us. I want to remind us that the journey is as important as the destination. The only thing that is ultimately real about your journey is the step you are taking right now. That's all there ever is. So it's important to keep your attention on the present. And to be sure that you are acting consistently with our vision, right now, each moment. It's in the richness of the journey where you find life's beauty.

Staying the Course

Sam and I had been seeing each other regularly for a while. I enjoyed his company. His quick wit made me laugh, and his inquisitive intelligence often gave me pause to think. When I introduced him to the children, he was friendly but took his cues from them regarding how involved he would be with our family. I was impressed and appreciative of his sensitivity to their needs. I also appreciated that he was interested in my work and, having read some of my writing for the marketing department, was quite encouraging. What surprised me was what little interest he had in the topic of vision and the conversations Jim and I were having. *Maybe it's because he's jealous of Jim*, I wondered. Finally, I asked him.

"Sam, I've noticed you seem disinterested when I talk about vision. When I bring it up, you listen for a few moments and then change the subject. I'm wondering why."

He hesitated a moment and said, "Ellie, I understand how important this is to you, but to be honest, I have a cynical attitude toward visioning. Ten years ago

I quit my job as a senior manager in a large corporation during a siege known as 'redeployment,' replete with vision and values workshops, many of which I was asked to lead. It was a farce. The company was downsizing, people were losing their jobs, and those who stayed felt bad for their friends and colleagues and insecure about their own jobs. The platitudes in the vision meant nothing. As a senior manager, I felt like we were trying to sell them a bill of goods instead of helping people deal with the reality of what was happening. Being part of the charade got to be too much for me, so I left."

I appreciated Sam sharing his experience with me. I had been so excited about vision that it hadn't occurred to me that there could be negative consequences if it was misused.

The next Tuesday on our morning walk, I shared Sam's comments with Jim.

Jim replied, "I don't think Sam's experience is all that unusual. This is why I wanted to understand vision before I did anything with the agency. I wanted to make sure that anything we did would be taken seriously. I think that if Sam's company had understood what we've learned about vision, things would have worked out differently."

"Understanding what we've learned would be helpful in most companies, but I'm not so sure in the case of Sam's company," I replied. "When Sam told me about his experience, it sounded like the people in his company were feeling hurt and betrayed. It reminded me of how my children had been feeling.

It was important that the first thing I did was listen to them, acknowledge their feelings, and understand their concerns. It was also important that I was willing to change. I think if I hadn't done those things first, they would have remained angry and resisted creating a family vision."

"Timing is important," Jim agreed. "As a leader, your people need to believe you are serious about the vision. If you've ignored some long-standing problems in the company, you might need to start by acknowledging the truth of the current realities, and maybe even take some action toward resolution before expecting people to trust your leadership enough to genuinely embark on the process of creating a shared vision."

Later, I shared these thoughts with Sam, and he agreed.

"Actually that's what Louis Gerstner did with IBM," Sam commented. "I was working for IBM when he took over. The company was a mess. It was losing billions of dollars a year. He didn't start with the vision. He started by making a series of quick changes to stop the hemorrhaging. There were huge layoffs. Fortunately, he didn't try to placate us with a vision, because it wouldn't have engaged us. But he was willing to assume strong leadership, and eventually we saw that he wasn't going to let us go under, which was reassuring. Then he got us focused on where we were going. Technology had changed and mainframes were obsolete, so we repositioned to respond to the need for a broad-based information technology integrator and focused on providing integrated solutions."

"Interesting," I mused. "Once again, I'm struck by how important timing is. Gerstner needed to first address the crisis, or they would have gone out of business. But if he had waited too long to create the vision, they would have gone out of business, because ultimately it was the vision that transformed them."

Sam smiled at me. "Ellie, my skepticism is waning. You've gotten me interested in vision."

The subject of getting knocked off course came up over our family dinner that evening. Jen told me about a movie she had seen in school about a young man named Terry Fox. I was so intrigued by what she said that later that evening I did an Internet search to learn more about him. I discovered the story of an amazing young Canadian who understood the power of vision and what happens when you get knocked off course.

While in high school, Terry was named Athlete of the Year. Shortly after graduation, he discovered he had a malignant tumor; his leg was amputated four days later.

The night before his operation, he read a magazine article about an amputee who ran in the New York marathon. That night, Terry dreamed about running across Canada.

During his follow-up treatment, Terry saw suffering as he'd never seen it before. He later wrote these words in a letter to the Canadian Cancer Society requesting their support:

> As I went through the sixteen months of the physically and emotionally draining ordeal of

chemotherapy, I was rudely awakened by the feelings that surrounded and coursed through the cancer clinic. There were faces with the brave smiles, and the ones who had given up smiling. There were feelings of hopeful denial, and the feelings of despair. . . . Somewhere the hurting must stop . . . and I was determined to take myself to the limit for this cause.

He left the cancer clinic with a vision to run across Canada to raise $1 million to fight cancer. There was a second purpose to his marathon: to demonstrate that there are no limits to what an amputee could do and to change people's attitude toward people with disabilities.

At first, Terry kept his vision a secret. He ran in the dark so no one could see him. When he felt confident that he could gain their support, he shared his vision with his family and close friends. Terry trained for fifteen grueling months, until he could run twenty-three miles a day. He took just one day off, Christmas, and only then because his mother had asked him to.

On April 12, 1980, he dipped his artificial leg in the Atlantic Ocean in St. John's, Newfoundland, to begin his run.

Terry became a national hero. He was greeted with cheers as he entered each town. People wept as he ran by with his fists clenched, eyes focused on the road ahead, and his awkward double-step and hop sounding down the highway.

He'd start before dawn every day, running in
shorts and a T-shirt printed with a map of Canada.
He didn't hide his disability. His artificial leg was fully
visible. Children were curious about his artificial leg.
How did it work? What happens when it breaks? He
encouraged them to ask questions and always stopped
to answer them.

The donations poured in.

Terry ran 3,339 miles from Newfoundland,
through six provinces. He was two-thirds of the way
home. He had run close to a marathon a day for 144
days straight. But on September 1, 1980, Terry had to
stop. He was sick. His cancer had recurred and had
spread to his lungs.

He flew home for treatment. And with his family beside him, Terry Fox died on June 28, 1981—one
month short of his twenty-third birthday.

Did Terry achieve his vision? I wondered. He didn't
complete his run. But then I thought again. His vision
wasn't to run across Canada. That was his plan to
achieve his vision. His vision was to raise $1 million
for cancer research and to increase awareness about
disabilities. In fact, he raised $23.4 million. And his
vision didn't end with his death. The Terry Fox Run
continues as a yearly event to this day and has raised
millions upon millions of dollars.

What happens when unforeseen events throw us
off course? Terry wasn't planning on a recurrence
of his cancer. It threw him off course, and his plans
changed. But his vision didn't.

I shared the story of Terry Fox and what I had learned about vision with Jim. I told him I believed that when unforeseen events throw us off course, we shouldn't try to get back on course. Instead, we should change our course—yet keep our focus on our vision.

• • •

"I've been thinking more about the role of goals," Jim mentioned during our next morning walk. "We decided that goals are the milestones that mark your progress toward your vision. So if you find yourself off course, as Terry Fox or IBM's Louis Gerstner did, then it's important to reset goals that are in line with your vision."

"Like sailing," I replied. Having grown up near Lake Michigan, I was an avid sailor. "When you're sailing on a lake, you keep your eye on your destination, but you don't point the boat directly at it. You want to catch the best wind to increase your speed. So you get to your destination by tacking—making a series of turns as you head toward your destination. You need to prepare for sudden shifts in the wind and be ready to change direction quickly, or your boat can tip. If you think of the destination as your vision, then tacking is when you set new goals."

"Good analogy, Ellie," Jim replied. "When we do our annual goal setting, now it will be in the context of our vision. And if something unexpected comes up midyear and we get knocked off course, we need to revisit our goals. It is like tacking."

"So if purpose is the what, picture of the future is the where, and values are the how, then goals should be the now," I said.

"I like that," said Jim.

We concluded that it's not realistic to expect to stay on course. Change is inevitable. The more important question is, What are you going to do when you find you're off course? If you can stay focused on your vision, you can reset your course. You might not be exactly *on course*, but you can *stay the course*.

I was struck by how important it is to stay consciously focused on your vision. A lot of people start out with hopes and dreams and live their lives believing they are on course, but one day they are startled to find that their lives are far from what they had wanted. And they have no idea how it happened. They just drifted off course slowly, pulled by tides and undercurrents so subtle they didn't even feel them. I realized how important it was to remain conscious of your vision. To be effective, visioning must be an ongoing process, not a one-time activity.

• • •

I've concluded that if you want to stay the course, it takes courage.

I really did have a talent for helping others understand and express their dreams. I had helped Jim, Marsha, and my family. But I wasn't doing it for myself. The work I did in the marketing department had further developed my skills and confidence in my writing, but the kind of writing I did for the job wasn't personally fulfilling. The longer I stayed with the insurance agency, the more restless I became.

This must be where courage comes in, I thought. It was clear that my personal vision meant using my talents in creative expression. Was I now going to take action? For me, action felt like jumping off a cliff. I didn't know where I would land. Would I be able to support myself if I left the insurance agency? Would I lose my connection with Jim? I knew what I really wanted. But I was afraid to take the next step.

One evening Jen said, "Mom, remember the stories you used to tell me at bedtime? They were great! You ought to write some of those stories."

Alex jumped in, "She's right, Mom. You're a natural storyteller."

My children inspired me. At home in the evenings, I began to write some of the stories I had told the children. And I changed them a bit to target them for adults by including messages about some of the things I had recently learned.

I thought more about my vision. It was about truth, not fear. It was about helping people act on their dreams—myself included. It was about allowing, not resisting. It was time for me to act on my vision.

I began writing in earnest in the evenings after work. I created a blog, and some of my stories were picked up by online magazines. Then I began pitching ideas for stories to newspaper and magazine editors and began earning money for my articles.

Having proven to myself that I could earn at least some money writing, I created a plan. The children would be leaving for college in a few months. Doug's parents were paying their tuition. Once they left, I could sell the house and move to a small apartment. I did a budget and decided I had enough savings to carry me for six months. I would devote those six months to seeing whether I could actually earn a living through writing. If not, then, well, I'd just have to see. I knew once I embarked on my journey, my trajectory was likely to change. What would be important would be to keep my sight on my vision at all times.

I discussed my plans with the children, who were quite supportive. They were willing to get part-time jobs while in college to pay for their spending money.

Jim told me that if I left the agency, I would be greatly missed, but he would understand. To my surprise and delight, he said he would like to continue our Tuesday morning walks.

One wonderful day, I gathered all my courage and took the leap. I knew it would be difficult at first, and it was. I had to adjust my lifestyle. At first I had only sporadic income from my magazine articles. The turning point came when Jim sent some of my articles to one of his college buddies, who was now the CEO of a large corporation. He needed help writing his biography. Jim's friend loved my writing and hired me! It was a short-term project but steady income. More important, my self-confidence as a writer increased. I began working on a book of my own for managers based on the lessons of childhood.

Sam was a wonderful support during this time. He read my articles and the various drafts of my book and was very encouraging. It meant so much to have him cheering me on. Although there were days I questioned whether I could actually make a living doing this, I knew I had made the right decision. Even though I would probably never be rich or famous, if I lived simply, I knew I would be able to earn a living doing what I loved. After all, I had heard it said that if you love what you do for a living, you'll never have to work a day in your life.

• • •

A year after I left the agency, my courage was challenged again. I had known Sam for several years. We had fallen into a comfortable relationship. He accepted me for who I was and what I gave him, never demanding anything else. Although I held something in reserve, he seemed to accept that also.

Unexpectedly, Sam was offered a wonderful job on the other side of the country. He asked me to marry him and go with him. I had no logical reason not to do it. I was in love with him, my children were no longer living at home, and I had a job I could do anywhere. The only reason not to do it was the biggest reason. Marriage was a huge commitment. I made a counteroffer: I would be willing to come stay with him for a few weeks every couple of months.

Sam confronted me. "I love you, Ellie. I know you love me. I also know you've been holding something back. It's time to let go. I'm moving and I want you to come with me, but only as my wife."

I hadn't seen Jim for a while. Our Tuesday morning walks had become infrequent. But I called him and asked whether he'd go for a walk with me that morning.

I told Jim about Sam's job offer and his desire to get married.

Jim asked me simply, "Are you in love with him?"

I replied, "Yes, but that's not the point."

"The way I see it, that's the only point," Jim smiled softly. "In our marriage, Carolyn and I have experienced a kind of love that is only available in the intimacy of commitment. Sam is offering you this gift, and it is a perfect fit with your vision."

Walking so comfortably with my dear friend Jim, I realized how much I had grown. I was drawn to what he described as the intimacy of commitment. I thought about my vision—it included seeking and sustaining loving relationships. By holding back on Sam, I had been limiting myself—and limiting the possibility of living my vision fully. At that moment my last wall went down, and I knew that I would have the courage to marry Sam.

From Success to Significance

With its vision guiding the agency over the next ten years, Carpenter Insurance tripled in size. The agency built a larger, beautiful building, opened offices in two other states, and developed a national reputation within the insurance industry. It was featured in several books, articles, and documentaries on topics such as "companies that have sustained great results" and "the best companies to work for."

As the agency grew, Marsha was appointed CFO and became a trusted advisor and confidant to Jim. Although it was a larger company and more complex in many ways, the vision continued to guide Carpenter, and the agency was able to maintain the culture by ensuring the values were lived. The performance review system included an evaluation not only of business results but also of the manager's ability to communicate effectively, develop a strong team, work collaboratively across department lines, and resolve conflict effectively. No one was promoted unless their behaviors were aligned with the company's values.

Living the values was considered as important as delivering business results. For example, a top-performing agent who brought in a lot of business could not get over his self-importance and develop cooperative working relationships with his peers. After receiving feedback from his boss and being provided coaching, his behavior did not improve. Although he was a top revenue producer, he was fired.

In one popular business magazine that featured the agency, one employee who was interviewed said:

> We are part of an industry that many people love to hate. But our customers don't feel that way at all. In fact, they respect us and are extremely loyal. We have incredibly low turnover, and we've grown continuously. How can that be? How can we be doing so well in this industry? It's because every single one of us knows and is committed to our vision. Our customers feel peace of mind, knowing they have financial security for worst-case situations. We establish personal relationships with each of our customers and understand their unique needs. They trust our integrity and competence to find them the right services and products at the best price, and if they have a problem, they know they only need to make one call—to us. If a stranger walked in off the street and asked, "What is your vision?" he would get the same answer from any person he asked—from the receptionist, to the agents, to customer service, to the custodian—not because we have memorized the words, but because we live them every single day.

As profits increased, Jim decided one good way to act on the company's value of "contributing to the success of the community and environment" would be to set up a foundation to provide education and resources to communities in developing countries. One of the employees at the agency was from a small village in Paraguay. The young man approached Jim to see if the foundation would help raise money to build a school in that region. The foundation decided to sponsor the project. Over the years, Jim and some others from the company visited the village and developed close, personal relationships with the mayor, the young man's father, and many of the people who lived in the community. Together they built an elementary school and later a high school and community center. They provided buses to transport children from remote locations to the schools. As the years progressed, it was obvious that education was making a significant difference in improving the economy and quality of life in the region.

Over the years, whenever he was asked when he was going to retire, Jim would reply, "Never!" However, his interest began to shift more and more toward the foundation. Eventually, Jim appointed Marsha as president of the agency, while he focused most of his attention on the foundation.

• • •

As for me, I applied the principles of vision that Jim and I had learned to my writing. I published a series of books for managers, titled *Mother Goose Management*, which took lessons of childhood stories and showed how they illuminated the principles of vision. My marriage with Sam was strong and fulfilling. He helped me stay connected with what was deeply meaningful and true. We had our ups and downs, but we were always able to work things out through the intimacy of our commitment.

One day, cleaning up files on my computer, I came across a folder that contained transcriptions of Jim's voice mail messages. Reading a few, I came across one that made me pause.

Good morning, everyone. This is Jim. Last night I was at a party with people that I haven't seen for a long time. It was just really fun.

I saw an old friend who had helped me get started in the business. I told him about our agency's vision and thanked him for the part he played in our success as a company and in my life. I could just see the beam and smile on his face.

The question I have for you today is: Is there anybody in your life who was there for you, and maybe you haven't thanked them lately? Maybe you haven't given them a hug. Have you kept your "I love yous" up-to-date, with your parents or other relatives, or friends, or people who were there for you way back?

I was inspired to send Jim a message telling him how much he had meant to me—how much he had influenced my life for the better. I thanked him and told him I wanted to keep my "I love yous" up-to-date. He had always been prompt in responding to me, and I was surprised that I didn't hear back from him within a few days—or at least get an acknowledgment that he had received my e-mail.

At the end of the week, I got a call that explained why.

"Ellie, this is Kristen. I wanted to let you know that Dad is in the hospital. I know he would want me to call you."

"Is it serious?" I asked.

Kristen hesitated. "I'm afraid it is, Ellie. It's his heart. He'd been feeling ill for about a week. Last night we had to rush him to the hospital."

"How bad is it?" I couldn't believe what I was hearing. Jim always seemed so strong . . . somehow invincible.

"There's really not much they can do for him," Kristen responded, her voice cracking for the first time in our conversation. "He's in the ICU, and the doctors didn't expect him to last the night. He's not conscious, but he's still with us this morning."

I hung up the phone and just stood there—completely stunned. How could someone with the biggest, strongest heart I'd ever known have a problem with his heart? It didn't make sense. All I knew was I needed to see him again, one last time. I didn't even know if he had read my e-mail, if I had kept my "I love yous" up-to-date with him. I called Sam to let him know what had happened and was on the next plane out.

I called Kristen as soon as my plane landed, expecting to go straight to the hospital.

"Don't go to the hospital, Ellie. Come to the house, okay?" she said gently and hung up the phone.

I sat numbly in the back of the taxi on the ride to Jim's house. Standing on the front step, I hesitantly rang the doorbell. Kristen opened the door. She didn't say a word. She just put her arms around me and started to cry. Tears filled my eyes. I couldn't fathom it. But I knew Jim was dead.

· · ·

After the funeral, we came back to the house. People were everywhere, telling stories about Jim—he had touched so many people in so many ways. After a while, I wandered down the hall toward the bathroom, passed Jim's study, and was immediately drawn in. It didn't even occur to me that this was a private space. I so strongly felt the need to connect with something of Jim. I walked to his desk, sat down, and looked out the window for a long time. This was the desk where Kristen had found Jim's obituary—his vision for his life. I glanced down and there on his desk—still open and looking as though it had just been read—was a printout of the e-mail I had sent. I breathed a sigh of relief. He had read it.

There was another sheet of paper on his desk. It contained some sketchy notes in Jim's handwriting. Apparently he was still leaving morning messages, and it looked like these were his notes for what would have been his next morning message.

I studied the words:

- what it means to move from success to significance
- the importance of giving back to your community
- we're all in this world together

I could almost hear him speaking. *Good morning, everyone. This is Jim.*

And so I said good-bye to Jim and thanked him for his last gift—the challenge to discover what it means to move from success to significance.

. . .

I've contemplated Jim's last message over the years, and I've come to the conclusion that on this planet, we are all part of one community; we all need to assume responsibility for creating a shared vision. If your vision is only about yourself and getting what you want, you are too narrowly focused. Ultimately, you may be successful in achieving your goals, but true satisfaction comes from having a significant impact and making a contribution.

The images we hold in our minds have a tremendous impact on the realities we create. I am concerned that there are so many images of destruction in movies, on television, and even in electronic games that children play. In contrast, there are so few images of what peace looks like. When I ask most people to describe what world peace looks like, they use vague terms. However, they are able to give quite vivid descriptions of what a post–World War III would look like. I've put a bumper sticker on my car that says "Visualize World Peace." And I look for any opportunity I can to help people create positive images for our planet.

In moving from success to significance, I discovered another underlying principle of vision:

The vision must benefit everyone it touches.

At the very least, acting on your vision must not cause harm to anyone. A vision for a company that benefits customers and not employees is useless. People have asked me whether Hitler had a vision. My response is "He was not aligned with the principles of vision as I describe them. But he had a charismatic personality and articulated a compelling image to those who would benefit from it. Unfortunately, it was at the expense of those it did not include and, as a result, millions suffered horribly."

Because the images we hold have the potential to manifest, we have a responsibility to take them seriously and to consider the larger community that is touched by our vision. My own vision has expanded to include a larger and larger scope. I'm confident that as my vision continues to expand, I'll recognize future opportunities to act on my vision as they arise, and that I will have the courage to act.

Thanks, Jim. Your vision was to have *made the world a better place by having been there*. It is. And I continue to move full steam ahead, my friend.

Creating Your Own Vision: Guidelines and Application

We hope you enjoyed *Full Steam Ahead!* In this section we've summarized the core concepts and tools from the story to help you create your own vision. Whether you are looking to develop a personal vision, a team vision, or an organization-wide vision, these principles will apply.

What Is Vision?

- Vision is knowing who you are, where you're going, and what will guide your journey.
- *Knowing who you are* means being clear about your purpose. *Where you're going* is your picture of the future. *What will guide your journey* are your values.

Why Is Vision Important?

- Good leadership starts with vision; leadership is about going somewhere.
- Vision helps you get focused, get energized, and get great results.
- Vision keeps you going during times of adversity.

Can a Team or Department Create a Vision When the Company Doesn't Have One?

Yes. Vision can start anywhere. You don't have to wait for the rest of the company. If you are a team leader, you can help your team create a vision. Others in the company will begin to notice the sparkle on your team and will become curious. Meanwhile, lobby your boss and your peer group to create a vision as well. In other words, look 360 degrees—down, sideways, and up.

The *Full Steam Ahead!* Model

There are two equally important aspects in creating a compelling vision: *content* and *process.*

 Content describes what the vision says. The three key elements that comprise a vision are *purpose, picture of the future,* and *values.*

 Process describes how to create, communicate, and live a vision. The story presents these aspects sequentially. In reality, creating a vision is not a linear process. As you clarify each of the elements of your vision, it is important to keep in mind the guiding principles of the Three Hows. Equally important to *what* your vision says is *how* it's created, *how* it's communicated, and *how* it's lived.

 The diagram depicts how the *process* influences the creation of the *content.*

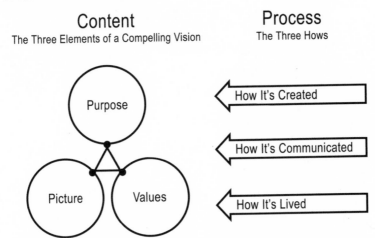

Content
The Three Elements of a Compelling Vision

Process
The Three Hows

Purpose

Picture

Values

How It's Created

How It's Communicated

How It's Lived

What follows is a "double-click" description that provides more information on each of the concepts depicted in the diagram.

Content: What It Says—The Three Elements of a Compelling Vision

Purpose

- Your reason for existence.

- Answers the question "Why?" rather than just describing your role or your activities.

- A deep and noble sense of purpose—a *significant* purpose—inspires excitement and commitment that makes work fun and helps you stay the course when things get tough.

Picture of the Future

- A picture of the end result; something you can actually see when you close your eyes. Not vague, such as "being great."

- Focuses on what you want to create, not what you want to get rid of.

- Is proactive, not reactive.

- Focuses on the end result, not the process for getting there.

Values

- Deeply held beliefs that certain qualities are desirable. They define what is right or fundamentally important and provide guidelines for choices and actions.

- Answer the question "How will you behave on a day-by-day basis?"

- Describe the behaviors that demonstrate what the value looks like when it is being lived.
- Need to be few in number and rank ordered in importance.
- Need to be consistently acted on or else are only good intentions.
- Personal values don't need to be exactly the same as those of your place of work, but they do need to be aligned in order for you to experience personal fulfillment.

A Compelling Vision

- Helps us understand what business we're *really* in.
- Has a significant purpose—is not solely about beating the competition.
- Provides a picture of the desired future that we can actually see.
- Provides guidelines that help us make daily decisions.
- Is enduring.
- Is inspiring—not expressed solely in numbers.
- Touches the hearts and spirits of everyone.
- Helps each person see how he or she can contribute.

Process: The Three Hows
How It's Created

- An honest and accurate assessment of the present is as important as a vision of the future.
  If you only have a vision, your head is in the clouds. If you only see your current realities, you are stuck in the mud.

- When you hold both your vision and the truth of your current reality, *creative tension* is generated. When you are willing to live with that tension without giving up on your vision, ultimately a shift occurs in favor of your vision.

- You don't have to wait for the company to have a vision. Vision can start anywhere—with one team or department or even with one individual.

- Use a collaborative, involving process that engages people in real dialogue about the vision and provides an opportunity to give feedback.

- When people have an opportunity to share their hopes and dreams, are involved in the discussions shaping the vision, and are included in making decisions, they have a clearer understanding of the vision, are more deeply committed to it, and move quickly to implement it.

- Although it is important to think through the consequences of major changes, it is also important to take some action that demonstrates leadership commitment.

How It's Communicated

- Visioning is an ongoing process; you need to keep talking about it.

- Once the vision is well understood, it can be condensed to a rallying call. However, the rallying call needs to emerge from a shared vision—it can't just be a marketing message.

- If you lose sight of the vision or stop acting in concert with it, the rallying call becomes meaningless and actually turns people off.

- It is important to share information on a regular basis to demonstrate that the vision is still the driving force.

- Help people interpret events and changes in light of the vision.

How It's Lived

- Set goals aligned with your vision.

- Learn from the past, plan for the future, and live in the present.

- Create supporting structures:
  - Set up processes and systems that are aligned with the vision and help people stay on track.
  - Align policies and procedures.

- First things first. If the ship is sinking, plug the holes.

- Leaders demonstrate their commitment by modeling the vision.

- Vision is a lot more than putting a plaque on the wall. A real vision is lived, not framed.

The following diagram depicts the "double click."

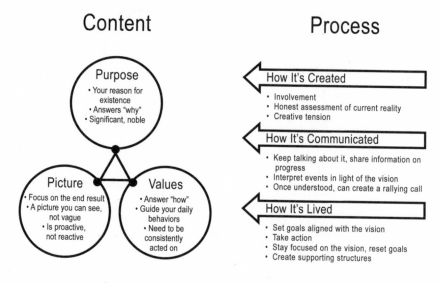

Guidelines for Staying the Course

- Keep the vision in mind whenever setting goals or doing strategic planning.
- Stay focused on the vision; change is inevitable.
- Be prepared to reset goals if you find you are off course.
- Take action. Once you have identified your vision, it is important to act consistently with it. It might be necessary to make small steps as you put plans and structures in place, but it's not possible to have it all planned out before you begin.
- Remember the Three Hows. Involve others, keep communications open, and demonstrate your commitment through your actions.
- Visioning is an ongoing process, not a onetime activity.

Test Your Team Vision

Here is a quick test to help you assess your team's vision. The scoring key that follows will help you evaluate and improve your team's level of development.

Rate your answer to each question as follows:

1 = Rarely
2 = Occasionally
3 = Sometimes
4 = Often
5 = Very frequently

____ Does everyone on your team share the same vision?

____ Does it excite, inspire, and motivate you?

____ Does it explain what business you are in?

____ Does it provide direction—create a clear picture of what you intend to accomplish?

____ Does it provide guidelines that help you make daily decisions?

____ Does it help you understand how your activities add value?

____ Does it help you identify priorities?

____ How often do you talk about purpose, where you are going, and/or values?

____ Is everyone deeply committed to achieving the vision?

____ Can each person see how they can make a contribution?

____ TOTAL SCORE

Vision Test Scoring Key

If your total score is . . .

45–50 Your team is *Mobilized*.

You have created a compelling vision that is energizing, provides focus, and sets direction. You are clear about where you are going and what values guide your journey.

Check it out and make sure others are as clear and as excited as you think they are.

Focus on how to create alignment and move your vision to reality. Refer to the chapters titled "How It's Lived" and "Staying the Course." When unforeseen events throw you off course, remember Terry Fox—revisit your vision and set a new course. Keep your vision alive. Act consistently with your vision in all ways, great and small.

39–44 Your team is *Forming*.

You have the beginnings of a powerful vision, but there is more work to be done. You need more clarity, more excitement, and/or engagement of others. Keep working on getting people aligned around the vision, and you will see an energized and focused workforce emerge.

Refer to the chapters titled "How It's Created" and "How It's Communicated." As you solidify your vision, test it against the benchmarks of a compelling vision.

30–38   Your team is *Typical*.

You live in a typical organization. Some people may be clear about where they are going, but there is no shared sense of direction. Although you may be accomplishing work, there is a lot of wasted effort. Work often needs to be redone because leaders change their minds or were not clear in their communications in the first place. People are juggling multiple concerns and trying to "do it all" because priorities are not clear.

Refer to the chapters titled "Element 1: Significant Purpose," "Element 2: Picture of the Future," and "Element 3: Clear Values" to learn how to craft the key elements of a compelling vision that will help your people get focused, get energized, and get great results.

29 or less   Your team is *Unfocused*.

If work is getting done, ask, "At what cost?" You and your people are in danger of burning out. Individuals may care deeply, but there is no collective mind-set or vision to align them around something greater than their daily tasks.

Refer to the chapter titled "What Is Vision, Anyway?" for an explanation of how vision accelerates both productivity and morale. When work is meaningful and connected to what we truly desire, we tap into a productive, creative power stronger than we ever imagined. It may be that some problems will need to be addressed first. Refer to the chapter titled "Staying the Course" for more information on this issue.

The Game Plan

The action steps described here are useful for teams such as:

- An entire team or department that wants to work together to create a shared vision
- A leadership team that wants to do initial planning on vision for a department or an entire company
- A facilitated large group that has come together to plan for their collective future
- A strategic planning group, as the first step in their process

Step 1: Create a Shared Vision

Have individuals and then the group reflect and agree on the fundamentals for each of the three key elements of a compelling vision. Agree on what is essential, but do not finalize the wording at this point, as it is important to be open to feedback from others outside the group.

Step 2: Honestly Describe the Current Reality

Examine your current realities in relation to your vision. Identify the strengths and weaknesses of your group in relation to your ability to achieve your vision. Develop plans for collecting additional information or verifying current perceptions. Understand the importance of the creative tension generated by holding the vision and being honest about the present.

Step 3: Develop Strategies to Move Forward

Identify the greatest opportunities to leapfrog forward. Identify what supporting structures are needed.

Develop bridging strategies to guide your movement forward. Also identify, and if possible make decisions on, "low-hanging fruit"—obvious problems that can easily be resolved without large repercussions. This demonstrates commitment to action.

Step 4: Plan for Involvement and Communication

Develop a plan to communicate the results of this meeting and to involve the rest of your department or organization in shaping the vision. Identify roadblocks and develop specific plans for action, including ongoing communications. If it is not possible to gather everyone at the same time, other processes can be used, such as holding a series of cross-company meetings. Whatever process is used to communicate the vision, the communication channels should remain open by engaging in a two-way process where the results of the discussions flow back to the senior leaders, who in turn then communicate their responses.

Step 5: Make Personal Commitments

Have individuals make personal commitments to specific goals and actions that demonstrate they are living and modeling the vision right now, even as they continue developing the vision.

Note: These steps, as well as the process to facilitate them, are described in more detail in *The Full Steam Ahead Field Guide*, available from The Ken Blanchard Companies. (See "Services Available" on p. 188.)

Acknowledgments

We would like to say a special thanks to the following individuals:

Steven Piersanti, president of Berrett-Koehler Publishers, for his excellent editorial advice, for urging us to write this second edition, and for creating an organization that exemplifies what our book teaches; **Jeevan Sivasubramaniam, Kristen Frantz, Maria Jesus Aguilo, Michael Crowley**, and all the rest of the folks at Berrett-Koehler for their enthusiastic support.

Martha Lawrence for her outstanding efforts and talent in assisting with the editing, proofing, and rewrites of multiple drafts. It has been a delight working with her.

Rose Mihaly, Don Carew, Wendy Christiansen, Chris Brunone, Gail Katz, Louise Klaber, Donna Mellen, Joan Stoner, Michele Kostin, and **Judd Hoekstra,** who read various manuscripts, for their detailed and very helpful comments and suggestions.

The many writers and pioneers in the field of management who have significantly influenced our thinking about the concepts in the book, especially **Drea Zigarmi** for his help in identifying the three elements of a compelling vision; **Peter Senge, Charles Kiefer,** and **Peter Stroh** for describing visionary organizations and the concept of structural integrity; **Warren Bennis, Marshall Sashkin, Barry Posner,** and **James Kouzes** for their studies of characteristics of visionary leaders; **Robert "Jake" Jacobs, Don Carew,** and **Fay Kandarian** for their work and commitment to collaborative processes; **Robert Fritz** for his thorough explanation of creative tension; and **Mary Parker Follett** for her contribution to the "law of the situation."

Finally, to those who allowed us to help in your journey, we thank you and extend our admiration. You have had the courage and the tenacity to make your vision a reality. Specifically, we would like to recognize **Nancy Maher,** executive vice president of TJX Europe; the late **Jim Lorence,** president of several divisions of The Stanley Works; and **Elizabeth Loughran,** former CEO of the Center for Human Development—courageous leaders we had the honor to work closely with over a significant period of time. We watched them go the distance, and by working with them, we learned a great deal about vision in action.

About the Authors

Ken Blanchard

Few people have impacted the day-to-day management of people and companies more than Ken Blanchard. A prominent, gregarious, sought-after author, speaker, and business consultant, Ken is universally characterized by his friends, colleagues, and clients as one of the most insightful, powerful, and compassionate people in the business world today.

From his phenomenal best-selling book, *The One Minute Manager* (coauthored with Spencer Johnson)—which has sold more than thirteen million copies and remains on best-seller lists—to the library of books coauthored with outstanding practitioners—*Raving Fans, Gung Ho!, Leadership and the One Minute Manager, Whale Done!*, and many others—Ken's impact as a writer is extraordinary and far-reaching. Ken is the chief spiritual officer (CSO) of The Ken Blanchard Companies, an international management training and consulting firm that he and his wife, Dr. Marjorie Blanchard, founded in 1979 in San Diego, California. He is also a visiting lecturer at his alma mater, Cornell University, where he is a trustee emeritus of the board of trustees. He is also a cofounder of Lead Like Jesus, a ministry devoted to helping people become servant leaders.

Ken and Margie, his wife of more than forty years, live in San Diego. Their son Scott and daughter Debbie hold key positions in the Ken Blanchard Companies.

Jesse Lyn Stoner

Jesse's first experience with the power of vision took place in a fifth-grade classroom, where she taught reading to children with learning disabilities. One day it occurred to her that the children had experienced so many years of failure, they probably couldn't imagine themselves reading a book. Experimenting with mental imagery techniques, she had the children visualize themselves reading. That year the children made more progress and were happier than any previous class. Intrigued by the children's success, Jesse went on to study the impact of vision in other settings. She wrote her doctoral dissertation on vision and leadership, and later identified the elements of an enduring vision.

For the past twenty-two years, as a business consultant and executive coach, Jesse has worked closely with leaders in organizations worldwide, ranging from large corporations to small start-ups and government agencies to nonprofits.

Jesse is the coauthor of several books, including *Leading at a Higher Level*, as well as *Benchmarks of Team Excellence*, a popular assessment that measures the extent to which a team shares a common vision and has developed the processes and skills to achieve it.

Founder and principal of Seapoint Center, Jesse resides in New England. To find out what Jesse is doing and thinking about right now, check out her blog at www.jessestoner.com.

Services Available

The Ken Blanchard Companies®

The Ken Blanchard Companies® is a global leader in workplace learning, productivity, performance, and leadership effectiveness that is best known for its Situational Leadership® II program—the most widely taught leadership model in the world. Because of its ability to help people excel as self-leaders and as leaders of others, SLII® is embraced by Fortune 500 companies as well as mid- to small-size businesses, governments, and educational and nonprofit organizations.

Blanchard® programs, which are based on the evidence that people are the key to accomplishing strategic objectives and driving business results, develop excellence in leadership, teams, customer loyalty, change management, and performance improvement. The company's continual research points to best practices for workplace improvement, while its world-class trainers and coaches drive organizational and behavioral change at all levels and help people make the shift from learning to doing.

Leadership experts from The Ken Blanchard Companies are available for workshops, consulting, as well as keynote addresses on visioning, organizational development, workplace performance, and business trends.

Tools for Change

Visit kenblanchard.com and click on "Tools for Change" to learn about workshops, coaching services, and leadership programs that help your organization create lasting behavior changes that have a measurable impact.

Global Headquarters

The Ken Blanchard Companies
125 State Place
Escondido CA 92029
www.kenblanchard.com
1.800.728.6000 from the United States
1.760.489.5005 from anywhere

Seapoint Center

Founded by Jesse Lyn Stoner, Seapoint Center uses the principles of *Full Steam Ahead!* to create engaged workplaces, where people enjoy work and achieve outstanding results.

Resources available:

- Information to more fully understand and apply the principles of *Full Steam Ahead!* at all levels: personal, team, department, and company-wide
- Examples of vision in action—real people who have used the principles of *Full Steam Ahead!* to succeed
- Access to tools to help implement *Full Steam Ahead!*

Services available:

- Facilitating teams in applying the principles of *Full Steam Ahead!* to take the team to a higher level
- Consulting with leaders to set the stage for change efforts or strategic planning
- Facilitating high-involvement meetings where a large group or an entire organization comes together to engage in real dialogue, define their collective future, and solve problems in real time
- Coaching individuals in creating a compelling vision for their work and/or personal life, identifying and eliminating barriers, determining goals and actions, and getting the support needed to keep moving *Full Steam Ahead!*

Tools to Create Vision

To learn about the materials, services, and resources to help you apply the lessons of *Full Steam Ahead!* to your company, team, and personal life, please visit:

Seapoint Center
www.seapointcenter.com

Social Networking

Ken Blanchard

Visit Blanchard on YouTube

Watch thought leaders from The Ken Blanchard Companies in action. Link and subscribe to Blanchard's channel, and you'll receive updates as new videos are posted.

Join the Blanchard Fan Club on Facebook

Be part of our inner circle and link to Ken Blanchard at Facebook. Meet other fans of Ken and his books. Access videos and photos, and get invited to special events.

Join Conversations with Ken Blanchard

Ken's blog, HowWeLead.org, was created to inspire positive change. It is a public service site devoted to leadership topics that connect us all. It is a social network, where you will meet people who care deeply about responsible leadership. And it's a place where Ken Blanchard would like to hear your opinion.

Ken's Twitter Updates

Receive timely messages and thoughts from Ken. Find out the events he's attending and what's on his mind *@kenblanchard*.

Jesse Lyn Stoner

Visit Jesse Lyn Stoner's Blog

Jesse's blog, JesseLynStoner.com, is where she explores current issues and shares her latest thinking. Jesse welcomes conversations and responds to all comments.

Join Seapoint Center on Facebook

For invitations to special events, access to videos and podcasts, and to find resources and examples of vision in action, join Seapoint Center at facebook.com/ SeapointCenter.

Follow Jesse Lyn Stoner on Twitter

Follow *@JesseLynStoner* to keep up with the latest news, find out what Jesse and her colleagues are doing and thinking, access relevant articles and videos, and enjoy food for thought.

Ken Blanchard and Mark Miller

The Secret
What Great Leaders Know and Do, Second Edition

The first edition of *The Secret* introduced a profound yet seemingly contradictory concept: to lead is to serve. Join struggling young executive Debbie Brewster as she explores this secret to truly motivating and inspiring people. Along the way, she learns why great leaders seem preoccupied with the future; why and how people on "the team" are invariably key ingredients of success or failure; what three arenas require continuous improvement; why true success in leadership has two essential components; how to knowingly strengthen—or unwittingly destroy—leadership credibility; and more. This second edition includes a section summarizing *The Secret*'s key points, making it even easier to use this book as a learning and development tool.

Hardcover, 144 pages, ISBN 978-1-60509-268-3
PDF ebook, ISBN 978-1-60509-470-0

Berrett–Koehler Publishers, Inc.
San Francisco, *www.bkconnection.com*   800.929.2929

Ken Blanchard, John P. Carlos, and Alan Randolph

Empowerment Takes More Than a Minute

Second Edition

Releasing employees' full potential and instilling a responsibility-oriented culture remains the best way to compete in a "do more with less" business climate. In this revised edition of one of the most effective business fables ever written, Blanchard, Carlos, and Randolph illustrate three keys that organizations can use to effectively tap into the knowledge, experience, and motivation power that people already have.

Paperback, 168 pages, ISBN 978-1-57675-153-4
PDF ebook, ISBN 978-1-60509-339-0

Ken Blanchard, John P. Carlos, and Alan Randolph

The 3 Keys to Empowerment

Release the Power Within People for Astonishing Results

Expanding on the three keys to empowerment presented in their bestselling *Empowerment Takes More Than a Minute*, Blanchard, Carlos, and Randolph provide a powerful set of actions to address issues that arise at all stages of the journey. This practical, hands-on guide provides the answers managers need to create a culture of empowerment—and achieve astonishing results—in their organizations.

Paperback, 304 pages, ISBN 978-1-57675-160-2
PDF ebook, ISBN 978-1-60509-340-6

BK Berrett–Koehler Publishers, Inc.
San Francisco, *www.bkconnection.com*   800.929.2929